UNBEARABLE AFFECT

WILEY SERIES IN GENERAL AND CLINICAL PSYCHIATRY

Series Editor
MAURICE R. GREEN
New York University
Medical School

UNBEARABLE AFFECT

A GUIDE TO THE PSYCHOTHERAPY OF PSYCHOSIS

DAVID A. S. GARFIELD

A WILEY-INTERSCIENCE PUBLICATION

JOHN WILEY & SONS, INC.

New York ▪ Chichester ▪ Brisbane ▪ Toronto ▪ Singapore

Copyright © 1995 by John Wiley & Sons, Inc.

All rights reserved. Published simultaneously in Canada.

Library of Congress Cataloging-in-Publication Data:

Garfield, David A. S.
    Unbearable affect : a guide to the psychotherapy of psychosis / by
David A.S. Garfield.
       p.   cm. — (Wiley series in general and clinical psychiatry)
    Includes index.
    ISBN 0-471-02536-4 (cloth : alk. paper)
    1. Psychoses—Treatment. 2. Affect (Psychology) 3. Emotions-
-Therapeutic use. 4. Psychotherapy. 5. Psychoses—Treatment Case
studies. I. Title. II. Series.
    [DNLM: 1. Psychotic Disorders—therapy. 2. Affect.
3. Psychotherapy—methods.   WM 200 G231u 1995]
RC512.G37 1995
616.89—dc20
DNLM/DLC
                                        94-44789

Printed in the United States of America

10 9 8 7 6 5 4 3 2 1

I am certain of nothing but the holiness of the heart's affections and the truth of imagination.

—*John Keats, Stanzas*

To the thousands of clinicians,
who provide meaningful therapy
to patients suffering with psychosis.

FOREWORD

This welcome, enticing, in many ways extraordinary book approaches the most difficult mental states in both usefully theoretical and practical human terms. It makes intelligible what is often dismissed as bizarre or unintelligible and, what may be most important, illustrates how these states can be managed and improved. It is a book of deep understanding and wise advice, moving, accurate, and useful.

The book is especially welcome now because the hope may well have passed that medications or hospitalizations will erase these states, however much they often help. Our streets show every day and to every passerby what still has to be done. Problems of self-esteem, social awkwardness, despair, and fury remain after all but the rare and most fortunate pharmacological results. Further, patients are many times reluctant to take medications or they stop before the medications are effective. We know that a good relationship between patient and helper is a principal ingredient securing all aspects of treatment. Such good relationships are especially difficult to create and sustain with the patients Dr. Garfield describes. He makes clear how they can be established.

In fact, the present era of chemical treatment has made the need for psychotherapeutic interventions all the more pressing. This is true not only because much must be done to support and supplement chemical aids, but also because medicines often bring patients past many of their symptoms to the point of needing to reconstruct their relationships and their work lives, building the viable existences they long despaired of achieving.

It is also a gift of Dr. Garfield's work that those curious about the meaning of psychoses and the light they shed on the human condition in general will find much here to ponder. Psychoses act like X rays, reducing the dense texture of ordinary life to its bare bones, the need for others, the dangers others present, the nature of psychological reality. Then we see a little more clearly what people require to construct those viable existences.

For practitioners and for mental health workers of all kinds, whether in hospitals, clinics, shelters, prisons, private practice, or wherever, Dr. Garfield offers incomparably much in the way of examples and advice. And for beginners as well as those contemplating a similar career, the book should be an *inspiration*, showing the way step-by-step toward the great work to be done.

LESTON HAVENS

Harvard Medical School
Cambridge, Massachusetts

PREFACE

When affect is used as a guide to psychotherapeutic work with patients in psychosis, the ordinary can emerge out of the extraordinary. Amidst the bizarre, the alien, and the unintelligible communications, the natural element of emotion provides the tool to guide both doctor and patient. By seeking out, harnessing, and rechanneling affect, the storms of psychosis can be successfully navigated.

Affect is the most fundamental element of the mind and brain. Like the physical elements of gravity, wind, and lightning, emotion has force and direction. As the great 19th-century Swiss psychiatrist Eugene Bleuler (Jung, 1907/1979) stated, "Thus, affectivity, much more than reflection, is the driving force behind all our actions and omissions." The neurobiologists know that the limbic system, also called the "primitive brain," is the home of affectivity. Psychologists, too, torn between the other basic ingredients of the psyche, such as thinking and volition, have given the nod to the primacy of affect. Bleuler (1911) stated it clearly when he declared, "Affectivity is the basis of life."

UNBEARABLE AFFECT

What happens when emotion becomes unbearable? We see it in the natural world—gravity and wind turn beautiful waters into hurricanes. Lightning strikes quickly destroy humans and forests alike. Little that is ordinary is left in the wake of natural disaster. So too, in psychotic patients, delusions, hallucinations, and incoherence are sometimes all that can be seen. The human being inside is left ravaged and little remains intact.

We are also aware that the most basic natural elements, when in turmoil, are not always explosive—at times they implode. The heat from the earth's core combined with the force and direction of gravity shifts the earth's underlying mantle; massive faults crack open to swallow up our usual existence. When human events build up and become too much to bear, emotion may implode, resulting in the negativism, the autism, and the paralysis of psychosis.

THE METHOD IN MADNESS

To attend to affect—to find it, make it tolerable, and place it back in its indigenous context is the goal of those who work with psychosis. This is the map first laid down by the late Dr. Elvin Semrad, a clinician-teacher-scholar at Harvard's Boston Psychopathic Hospital/The Massachusetts Mental Health Center. Semrad stood on the shoulders of Bleuler and Jung in his emphasis on affect as the organizing principle in psychosis. No doubt, Semrad would have agreed completely with the words of the European psychiatrist, Godferaux (Jung, 1907/1979), "Below the cold and rational laws of association of ideas, there are others which conform more to the profound needs of life. This is the logic of feeling." The affect approach to psychosis is a psychoanalytic approach. And yet, those who work with psychosis know that any successful approach must also be psychosynthetic. Does conflict bring about psychosis or do defects? With emotion as the guide to healing psychotic patients, clinicians can see how internal emotional strength makes bearing unbearable affect possible. Conversely, by diminishing the affective intensity of conflict, the patient's internal condition is less twisted out of shape.

Neuropsychiatry and psychopharmacology have made great strides in the management of psychosis. Research in phenomenological neuropsychiatry has resulted in brilliant discoveries concerning the neurological components of psychopathology. Research on the cerebellar contributions to thought disorder (Taylor, 1991), on the role of language centers (Cleghorn et al., 1992) in hallucination, and cortical-subcortical circuits (Cummings, 1985) in delusion, all make the phenomena of psychosis better understood in their brain basis. Psychopharmacology too, has made major advances in quieting the storms of psychosis. Newer antipsychotic medications, novel uses of anticonvulsants, and electroconvulsive therapy can rapidly diminish psychotic symptoms.

Yet, neurobiology and psychopharmacology are like ocean sonography and better fiberglass boats. They give precise indications of the terrain and they provide better equipment for the hurricane-force winds. But they do not show you a way out; nor do they chart the course.

Semrad's map out of psychosis focuses on finding the affect in the psychosis, bringing it into the patient's body and, finally, putting it into words in the context of the life history of the patient. His blueprint is crucial but incomplete. Semrad begins with acknowledgment—the finding of affect, locating it in the delusional, hallucinatory, or neologistic elements of psychosis—and having the patient "own" the affect. This is a good start. Semrad's second step, "bearing affect" is a complex affair. It requires more than bringing the unbearable affect in psychosis into the patient's body. Added onto Semrad's plan is the idea that a special kind of relationship with the therapist is required. Here the clinician is not only the copilot, but also serves as the patient's own missing eyes, ears, and hands. The therapist becomes, in some respects, a living part of the patient's experience.

Finally, Semrad's design calls for putting that which was unbearable affect into a new perspective. As affect is better tolerated in the body, it can now be tied to the rational mind. A better emotional understanding of his or her history is not enough for the patient. Remobilization, revitalization, and further development of the patient's own affectivity must be active, ongoing occurrences.

STRUCTURE OF THE BOOK

The format of the book is a bit unconventional. It chronicles the development of a young psychiatric resident, Tony Potter, as he learns to work with a few psychotic patients. The character of Dr. Potter represents a composite of myself and several psychiatric residents I have supervised. Each chapter begins with the next sequel of Dr. Potter's work with one of the book's selected patients. The patients described in the book are based on actual cases. One of the patients is a composite; identifying information about the others has been altered to preserve confidentiality. The second part of each chapter includes the theoretical underpinnings of the lessons that Dr. Potter has learned in this particular therapeutic encounter. The third part of each chapter is addressed directly to the readership of the book with further illustrations of the main points or techniques of the chapter. It is my hope that this structure will aid readers in entering "the storm," and gaining both an empathic and technical understanding of the centrality of affect in psychosis.

The book is divided into three sections. Section I, "Affect Diagnosis," includes four chapters that address finding and understanding unbearable affect in the initial clinical work with psychosis. Chapter 1 introduces the book's main character, Dr. Tony Potter, in his first encounter with a psychotic individual. Unbearable affect can be seen in this vignette as being the focal point around which psychosis turns. Chapter 2 demonstrates the utility of and techniques for extracting affect from the patient's first communications. Chapter 3 looks at the precipitating event that brought the patient to clinical attention. A specific feeling tone is embedded in the scene of the precipitating event; in psychosis, that feeling affect is unbearable. Chapter 4 brings the clinician inside the mental machinery of the patient to see how primary mental processes transform affect into the bizarre forms of psychosis.

Section II of the book, "Affect Therapeutics," consists of five chapters that deal with concepts and techniques specific to mobilizing and transforming affect in the therapeutic relationship. Chapter 5 deals with the initial way in which therapists help patients contain unbearable affect. This is a new view on countertransference. Chapter 6 concerns "The Forms and Transformations of Affect." As affect moves out of psychotic forms, where does it go? This chapter outlines techniques for facilitating the transformation of affect. Special techniques for handling certain types of psychosis are illustrated in Chapter 7, "Shame, Pride, and Paranoid Psychoses." Persecutory states can be particularly tricky to deal with, and several clinical suggestions are offered. Chapter 8 speaks to the specific ways in which patients lost in the storms of psychosis need the therapist. Here, the notion of clinician as selfobject and the subsequent impact of affectivity is introduced. In effect, the therapist must become the missing eyes and hands of the patient/pilot disabled by psychotic turmoil. Chapter 9, "Bearing Unbearable Affect," the final chapter of Section II, points out how and why it is essential that patients make contact with the emotionality of the clinician.

Section III of the book, "A Life's Work: Staying Out of Psychosis," presents ideas and approaches geared toward the development of self and affect and the means for staying out of psychosis. Chapter 10, "Putting Emotion in Perspective," illustrates how healthy emotional change results in the patient's enlisting new "crew members" who help bear difficult affect-laden situations. Chapter 11, "Staying Out of Psychosis," the book's final chapter, reviews theories of change in the psychotherapy of psychosis and contrasts them with the affect-centered approach. It also addresses the issue of posttreatment access to the therapist.

FINDING THE EXTRAORDINARY WITHIN THE ORDINARY

The central role of affect in both conflict and deficit in the psychotherapy of psychosis is emphasized throughout the book. A dual therapeutic process is outlined. First, the extraordinary phenomenon of psychosis is taken back into the ordinary discourse of emotion. Most often, psychosis leaves little in its wake. It is also essential to discover those unique, unexpected, and extraordinary capacities that lay hidden within the bland, almost absent, ordinary elements of the patient's person. As the burden of unbearable affect is diminished, the emotional capacity of the patient is broadened. The task is not simply to get out of harm's way. The task is to be of assistance until one's presence on board is no longer needed. This is the rechanneling of affect. These transformations become visible when the patient's grandiose delusions are replaced by actions of bravery or when a legacy of mutism may find a later, unexpected outlet in poetry.

DAVID A. S. GARFIELD

The Chicago Medical School
North Chicago, Illinois

ACKNOWLEDGMENTS

Recognizing the great number of people who have inspired, supported, and encouraged the development of this book is no small task. I am grateful for the fellowship and support of my friends and colleagues in the International Symposium for the Psychotherapy of Schizophrenia. I am deeply indebted to the students of the late Dr. Elvin Semrad, who diligently taught and worked at the Massachusetts Mental Health Center and, in particular, the late Dr. Doris Menzer Benaron. Dr. Leston Havens has been and continues to be a wonderful friend and advisor/mentor. I am continuously inspired by the original members of the Forum for the Advancement of the Psychotherapy of Psychosis (FAPP) including Drs. David Green, Carolyn Manson, Chris Morse, Jill Robertson, Jeff Rossman, David Mann, and Haviva Goldhaar. I am grateful for the support of Drs. Marion Tolpin and Ernest Wolf. This book would not have been possible without the encouragement of my wife, Dr. Bonnie Garfield and also of Dr. Robert Garfield, Jack Neems, Jake Krieger, and Dr. Richard McKnight. Jacob, Jenny, Deborah (Wunnicke), Harriet, and Milt Garfield have been patient with my time away from family in the preparation of this book. Drs. Fred Sierles, Nutan Atre-Vaidya, and Michael Taylor in the department of Psychiatry and Behavioral Sciences at FUHS/The Chicago Medical School have provided time and support for my interests and writing. Kelly Franklin of John Wiley & Sons was an invaluable aid in her comprehensive editing, hand-holding, and advising. Nancy Cannon and Barbara Fischel graciously contributed numerous hours typing this manuscript.

D.A.S.G.

CONTENTS

SECTION III   A LIFE'S WORK: STAYING OUT OF PSYCHOSIS

SECTION I

AFFECT DIAGNOSIS

1

INTRODUCTION: THE FOCAL POINT

The Focal Point: Andrew Scott Stevens

Although Tony Potter's first encounter with psychosis occurred while he was in medical school, it came in a nonmedical way. He had, like countless others, noticed the old bag ladies and the scrawny young men near Washington Square Park who walked about mumbling to themselves. They all wore torn and dirty clothes that never seemed to fit. The elderly, short women in the park fiercely guarded their turf; no one should get too close to their garbage bins nor their shopping carts. One rather heavy old woman lay sprawled along the entire length of a bench. Though her head never moved, her eyes never closed. Tony could feel her gaze on him as he jogged through the park. These were the homeless mentally ill. New York absorbed them effortlessly. Like everyone else, Tony avoided them, steered around them, picked up his pace as he strode past them. But one afternoon on his regular running route, an odd thing happened. He had circled back through Soho and as he was passing the new "all-white" antique and kitchen store (white tables, white chairs, white coffeepots, etc.), he found that he was running alongside an athletic-looking man who appeared to be about 30 years old.

"All white—but they don't discriminate on the basis of color—only on the basis of net worth," the runner said. Tony nodded in agreement and chuckled. Soho was not what it used to be. Still dirty, still dilapidated in many parts, but not at all inexpensive.

"How far are you going?" Tony asked.

"My usual 10 miles," the runner replied.

The runner, Andrew Scott Stevens, lived in the Village with his parents. His "usual 10" was much longer than Tony's daily jog; Andrew started up near the Strand bookstore and ran down through the East Village before circling around and back. He had run in the New York Marathon. Tony was impressed. His own routine was now 5 miles, he had run 10 on occasion but never on a regular basis. They ran at the same time each day and began to look for each other when they were out. Tony never said it, but the idea that maybe he could get to the point where he could run the marathon hid in the back of his mind. Running with Andrew was a terrific way to head there without having to think much about it.

It was after the third or fourth time that they had been out that Tony started to get the feeling that all was not exactly right with Andrew Scott Stevens. Andrew was always rubbing his left elbow even though he claimed that there was nothing wrong with it. Sometimes, as they would approach the end of a block, Andrew would suggest that they cut to the left at the corner. At first, Tony thought that he was just trying to vary the route. But Andrew remarked that it was Jones Pizza or number 99 First Avenue that he was trying to avoid. Later, the muscular 30-year-old would start talking about a certain policeman, Donald Jones. It was Donald Jones, Badge 99722—NYPD, who had answered the call to the Stevens's apartment that first time he had been taken to the psychiatric ward at Bellevue.

Ten years earlier, Andrew had just started his freshman year at Columbia. He lived at home. He had wanted to live in the dorms but it was impossible. His parents didn't want him to—they couldn't afford it. His father needed his help around the apartment building and encouraged Andrew to save money for graduate school. There were plenty of excuses as to why he had to stay at home. At the same time, Bernard Scott Stevens, Andrew's father, would tell his son that a man should be independent. "Don't let anyone tell you what to do. Be your own man." That was the spoken word.

The father's life story was not one of success. He probably was lucky to have stumbled onto the job of being the superintendent of a large luxury apartment complex in the East Village and luckier yet to have had a brilliant son like Andrew. All A's in all his classes in junior high school and high school—and the class Valedictorian as well. Bernard Stevens had every right to be proud of his son; instead, he was jealous and never missed an opportunity to berate the boy. Conversely, Andrew had always admired his dad—the way everyone in the building depended on him and how his dad always seemed to stand tall. Although he winced under the constant barrage of criticism, it almost increased the intensity of his love for and loyalty to his father.

In that first year at Columbia, things changed abruptly. Andrew discovered girls. There was a lovely young woman, Susan Solere, in his freshman calculus class. She liked him. He started to spend time with her after class; they would take the subway and go to the small coffee shops in the Village and talk for hours. Susan was smart. She was principled. She believed in the power of the mind to create, and she believed in the power of the heart to change things. She believed that New York City could be freed from the power of gangs and drugs and fast money, if people would only take responsibility for their own destiny. Susan was someone to believe in, and Andrew Stevens believed in her.

The heat turned up at home. Andrew's mother complained that he stayed out too late; there were chores to do around the apartment. Was he turning into a spoiled college brat? His father was not particularly interested in hearing about this Susan Solere—she sounded like an "irresponsible, wishy-washy pseudointellectual radical." As Andrew's protests in her defense mounted, so did the pressure on him to remain at home. Andrew had hoped that since his folks were doing reasonably well financially and since he had a sizable scholarship to Columbia, they would reconsider the possibility of his moving into the dorms. Susan lived in the dorms at Barnard.

They laughed at him and told him that he was dreaming—that he had no idea of how much it cost to live in New York City and that they didn't even know if they could supplement any of his Columbia education. Andrew became distraught and then agitated. He tried to argue rationally with them, but his father became less and less communicative and his mother kept telling him to be realistic.

Andrew became confused, he had no idea what to believe. His parents had worked hard to give him the best—he knew they were not wealthy like many of the people who lived in the building. And yet there was Susan. How he loved her! Yet, he couldn't tell her about his home life. She wouldn't understand that it was different for him. He stopped meeting her after class. At home he became despondent and withdrawn. He would take out the trash to the large dumpsters but forget to unload them. He started jogging: Sometimes he would run until he became lost, and it would take him hours to come home. He missed classes. One evening after going to calculus class he spotted Susan on the way out. She called over to him but he ducked out the door and started running. He ran all the way home—it was miles and miles and he didn't even have his running shoes. He arrived late in the evening. Out of breath and in a half-trance, he walked into the main lobby. There in the spacious hallway, he peered into the large mirror that covered one entire wall. It had 40 separate panels and together they formed a reproduction of Michelangelo's vision on the ceiling of the Sistine Chapel; Adam reaching out to touch God's outstretched hand.

When the doorman finally realized that something inside was wrong, only 10 panels remained. The boy's fists were moving so fast that he couldn't tell what was causing the panels to shatter. Yet, the shattered glass and mirror were streaked with blood. Someone had called the police and the officer who arrived, Donald Jones, was unaware that there might be a medical emergency until he noticed the dark stain under the young man's sweatshirt. Andrew had tucked his hands up under his sweatshirt and continued to stand and stare at what was left of the mirrors.

Mr. Stevens had been paged and he and his wife were standing next to their son in utter confusion. Jones quickly noticed that the boy was disturbed and insisted that Andrew come with him to the hospital. His father, Bernard Stevens, became hysterical:

"There's nothing wrong here, officer. Just an accident," he said.

"Sir," Jones replied, "the boy appears to be hurt and I think I had better get him to a hospital."

"What are you talking about? Andrew's not hurt—he's fine. Can't you see that? You're fine aren't you?" He prompted the boy.

"Sure, I'm fine," Andrew responded.

"But your hands are a mess. And this place is a mess." Jones emphasized.

"A crowd was gathering in the lobby and several tenants were whispering about Andrew.

"I'm afraid he'll have to come with me, sir. I'll see to it that he gets help and you're free to follow me in your car if you wish," the policeman offered.

"You can't do this. You can't do this. You can't do this!" The father was beside himself. He laced his arm through Andrew's.

"I'm afraid I have no choice," replied the officer, as he struggled with the father for control of the boy's body. He finally yanked Andrew away by the elbow and led him outside to the patrol car.   ✦

UNBEARABLE AFFECT

There are countless other examples of unbearable affect with which the students of psychosis are all too familiar. At some point, feelings mount until they become too much to bear. In many cases, it is one feeling at the center; in others it is a mixture. To work effectively with patients in psychosis, clinicians must be able to "get a handle" on what it is that moves the patient. Where is the focal point?

This book is about emotion and psychosis. It is meant for clinicians and students; its intent is to anchor the reader in a therapeutic approach to the patient. At the heart of this approach is unbearable affect. In the preceding case, Andrew Stevens bends, hides, and runs until he is no longer able to avoid his dilemma. The anguish he feels at the sight of his lost love/last hope, and the subsequent rage at his psychological subjugation can no longer be contained. With his fury, we approach the focal point. Donald Jones becomes a pawn in the emotion's drama. At the center of it is rage and despair with nowhere to go.

The affect approach to psychosis owes a great debt to the late Dr. Elvin Semrad (Khantzian, Dalsimer, & Semrad, 1969; Semrad & Van Buskirk, 1969), a revered analyst at the old Boston Psychopathic Hospital (The Massachusetts Mental Health Center), whose writings and teachings articulated a pathway to psychological healing for those with psychotic illness. Many of Semrad's trainees have been inspired by his commitment to working with psychotic patients and, particularly, by his adage of "acknowledge, bear, and put in perspective" the unbearable affect that has driven the patient crazy. There are many schools of theory within psychoanalysis including the classical, object relations, interpersonal, existential, and self psychology viewpoints. Within each set of theories and techniques, emotion plays an essential role and each school affords it significant power in its theory (Krystal, 1982; Lichtenberg, 1992). In this approach, with affect as the pivot point, the clinician is freed up from the constraints of a multitude of sometimes conflicting theoretical views.

THE HISTORY OF AFFECT AND PSYCHOSIS

The academic giant of 19th-century psychiatry, Emil Kraepelin (1903), was one of the first scholars to categorize the psychoses into two basic types: manic-depressive illness and dementia praecox (schizophrenia). In addition, he delineated three fundamental dimensions of the mind—emotion, cognition, and will. Kraepelin described how these three areas are affected in each of these illnesses. Here, in this book, from Kraepelin's tripartite mind, emotion is selected to be the crucible of psychosis rather than cognition or will. Along with a disturbance in attention, Kraepelin was impressed with the dementia praecox patient's affective state. In terms of emotion, he noticed "First, the poverty or superficiality of emotional reactions; second, their incongruity with the ideational content dominating the psyche at the time" (Jung, 1907/1979, p. 19). Almost all of Kraepelin's students came to the conclusion that affect and affectivity were at the basis of mental life.

Eugene Bleuler, author of the classic monograph "Dementia Praecox or The Group of Schizophrenias," argued: "Thus, affectivity, much more than reflection, is the driving force behind all our actions and omissions. It is likely that we act only under the influence of pleasure/unpleasure feelings; our logical reflections get their power only from the affects associated with them." "Affectivity is the broader concept of which volition and connation are only one aspect" (Jung, 1907/1979, p. 38). Here, Bleuler believes that affect is even more central to mental life than the other two parts of Kraepelin's tripartite mind—volition (will) and connation (cognition). Throughout time, there has been something compelling about feelings.

EMOTION, THEME, AND PSYCHOSIS

Like many gifted clinician-teachers, Semrad depended on the physician-scholars who came before him. Carl Jung's (1909/1979) theories had a profound impact on Semrad's work. During a time of great excitement and discovery in psychiatry, Jung worked as a junior clinician/scholar at the famous Burgholzi mental hospital in Zurich. Following in the footsteps of his mentor, Eugene Bleuler, Jung felt that an affective theme nearly always lay at the heart of the psyche's woes. He described this premise as the "feeling-tone complex." He developed this concept after conducting a series of word association experiments in the early 1900s. The odd productions of psychotic patients could be understood by concentrating on the focal point of emotional theme.

Jung emphasized that what distinguishes the organization of madness from that of sanity is that it is constellated around a particular emotion rather than by logical premise. Thus, delusions, hallucinations, or loose associations (non sequiturs) have at their core a distinctive, traceable thread of a specific affect. There are no "crazy" delusions, hallucinations, or loose associations, but rather angry, jealous, sad, or scary ones. Out of each of these manifestations of psychosis, a feeling-toned theme can be selected that aids the clinician in translating the patient's behavior into logical, consensual, speech (secondary process).

Jung went on to posit how specific "laws of association" draw in the particles of everyday experience to this feeling-toned complex like iron filings to a magnet. These laws of association included the law of (1) similarity (things are connected to each other via having similar attributes), (2) coexistence (things are connected to each other via being in the same place at the same time or by following one another immediately in time), (3) verbal-motor combination (things are connected to each other because one thing sounds like the other thing behaves), and (4) sound combination (things are connected to each other because their names sound alike). Examples from the preceding case include Andrew Stevens's elbow or the policeman's name and badge number—Jones, 99722. Conversely, Jung proposed, the feeling-toned complex might propel the items of experience forward. Michelangelo's mirrored scene shatters under the force of the unbearable affect.

Not all cases of psychosis dramatize the shattering of the psyche as vividly as the Stevens case. Often, psychopathology surfaces out of more subtle scenarios; sometimes they are impossible to elicit. Nonetheless, the emotional content is almost always visible in some form, whether it takes shape in the illumination of past events, current events, or the transference relationship to the clinician. By focusing on the theme of the patient's communication, the clinician can avoid the pitfalls of logical inquiry—confusion, frustration, and worse, disconnection. As Shakespeare's (1968) Polonious commented on Prince Hamlet: "Tho' this be madness, yet there is method in't." The method organizing madness is not logical, it is emotional.

AFFECT IN THE BODY

Andrew Stevens's elbow is pulled into his psychosis as he is taken from his family of origin (by the elbow) by patrolman Jones, and it is important for the student of psychosis to note the role the elbow plays as a day-to-day reminder. When he is running, he rubs it. The clinician may want to know—is it irritated? Does it burn? One of Semrad's crucial contributions to the study of psychotic experience was his emphasis on the physical "location" of feelings.

Spitz (1957), Sharpe (1940), Freedman and Grand (1976) and, recently, McDougall (1989) and Siegelman (1990) have emphasized the important communicative link between affect and its symbolic representation in bodily sensation. It comes as no surprise that along with the cognitive-ideational components of affect (sad thoughts) and the perceptual aspects (sad voices) of affect, that the "feeling" or bodily experiential aspects of affect are also of key importance and persist into adulthood. Thus, *feelings* are *felt somewhere* in the body. Grief becomes a "lump in the throat" or a heaviness in the chest ("heavy heart"). Anger becomes a churning in the stomach or heat sensations in the arms, neck, head, and face ("my blood was boiling"). Semrad used this tie extensively in helping psychotic patients reconstitute. What role would Andrew's elbow play in his psychotherapy? Will it be a lightning rod for his irritation in general?

MENTAL PROCESSES

Delusional perceptions, auditory hallucinations, neologisms, and non sequiturs have been identified as the defining criteria for psychosis (Bleuler, 1905/1950; Kraepelin, 1903), and these psychopathological phenomena have also spawned generations of writers and researchers drawn to explain the "unnatural." Armed with the tools of their respective trades, psychiatrists, psychologists, cognitive scientists, neurologists, aphasiologists, linguists, and even artificial intelligence computer researchers have put forward their explanations. Here, too, affect has played an important role.

Inappropriate affect, flat or blunt affect, emotion-driven primary process, affective responses to unstructured stimuli, affect recognition, developmental levels of affect, disturbances in prosody (emotional coloring of speech), paucity of affect words, affective word sounds and morphology, and emotion profiles in the text of psychotic speech are all testimony to the crucial role that affect has been seen to play in psychosis. Is emotion physiological? How does it locate itself in the body? Does emotion give shape to recognition? Can emotion configure perception? There is evidence to support all these contentions (Lane & Schwartz, 1987). In Andrew's case, it was the rage that burst forth, but was it sadness that was truly the unbearable affect? Perhaps, intolerable emotion sits like an abscess, loculated off, sparing the rest of the personality but intermittently provoking secondary, mental effects.

AFFECT IN THE THERAPEUTIC WORKPLACE WITH PSYCHOTIC PATIENTS

Much has been written concerning the unique kinds of experiences that therapists of psychotic patients encounter (Garfield, 1987; Searles, 1965; Winnicott, 1947). The empathic process itself in the psychotherapy of psychotic patients may need to be entirely revamped in this regard. Empathy has most often (Greenson, 1960) been viewed as a kind of affective attunement, and thus, the clinician places his or her affective state in resonance with the patient's. If the patient's affect is unbearable, what must it be like for the clinician?

As the focal point of emotion moves between patient and doctor, much can be gleaned from its forms and transformations. Savage (1961) described his work with a frustrating patient, who constantly complained of a toothache, although his dentist could find no physical cause. The analyst became progressively annoyed at his patient's host of complaints and demands, and at the patient's rejection of help.

Taking refuge behind the analytical silence, I let myself ruminate about the question of my annoyance with him, not an easy thing to do because of the persistent, nagging quality of his complaints. It gradually dawned on me that he was denying me useful material for analysis, he was not giving me any evidence of progress and thus, he was reactivating all my personal conflicts about oral frustrations. It finally occurred to me that he was complaining of the same thing in me, that I was frustrating him in the transference just as his mother has subjected him to severe oral frustration. This turned out to be the case. His toothache disappeared.

Affect can be contagious (Furer, 1967). One frequently bears witness to the illogical spread of laughter or the way in which sadness can envelop a room of strangers. In psychotherapy, this contagious quality puts the clinician at risk for being at the receiving end of intense emotions. Countertransference pitfalls with hallucinating and/or delusional patients have been well documented (Modell, 1980; Rosen, 1968; Searles, 1979). Paying close attention to one's own emotional reactions becomes not only a useful informational tool but an important requirement for treatment stability. As emotion is mobilized, processed and integrated, there are times when its fluidity can be perilous. When the psyche is overwhelmed, the motor system may absorb affect and harmful or deadly actions can occur. Noticing warning signs, finding emotional resting places and discerning the best ways to jointly bring the intolerable into safe and hopeful misery define the tasks of this transformation of emotion from psychosis to recovery. With Andrew Stevens, keeping him alive may become the central long-term goal as unbearable affect is made bearable.

PUTTING THE PIECES BACK TOGETHER AGAIN

Feeling good about oneself may make it a lot easier to feel. Affect provides the glue for the developing self (Stolorow & Stolorow, 1987). If certain emotions are segmented or sent off, then certain parts of the psyche become unavailable for full participation in the life of the individual. Affect mastery and self-esteem are closely allied.

Assessing sources of self-esteem is vital to the recovery from psychosis. A trusted clinician becomes a central wellspring in this regard. Notions of the auxiliary ego (Arieti, 1955), the therapist as transitional object (Rosenfeld, 1965), the formation of a therapeutic symbiosis (Searles, 1979), and the therapist as selfobject (Kohut, 1971) speak to the recurrent clinical finding that someone must help the patient bear the untenable. The scaffold of mental life must be buttressed or the foundation will break under the weight of the emotional demands. A renowned Chicago psychoanalyst, Franz Alexander coined the expression, "the corrective emotional experience" (Alexander & French, 1946).

He believed that the job of the therapist was to provide the emotional nurturing that had been defective during the patient's early upbringing. Perhaps, Alexander's phrase is apt even if significant disagreement exists as to what really is "corrective" in psychotherapy. Few have argued that emotional experience in psychotherapy is unnecessary.

Repair of psychosis and its behavioral manifestations occurs through a process of "acknowledging, bearing and putting in perspective" (Semrad & Van Buskirk, 1969), the intolerable affective themes left unresolved from childhood that again overwhelm the patient's ego. This framework of psychotherapy with psychotically disturbed patients represents, in essence, a modification of Freud's (1914/1958) recommendations in "Remembering, Repeating, and Working Through." In this modification, affect serves as the "handle" that the psychotherapist "grabs" in the effort to help the patient tolerate unbearable feelings and, subsequently, to reorganize his or her behavior in interpersonally productive ways.

The therapist begins with the precipitant (the presenting chief complaint) that has brought the patient to treatment most recently and seeks to help the patient tolerate that which is overwhelming. The therapist and patient then work backward, at the patient's pacing, to establish what may be called an "affective road map of the past." With some stability in the present and with some hope for the future, the past now rolls out; an unraveling takes place. Each earlier, unresolved scene comes into focus colored with intense sadness or anger: Andrew's pride in his father and sadness at the lack of attention from him; Andrew's wish to please the old man and the impossibility of the task; his mother's complicity in keeping him under the family's thumb. In myriad memories, the specific scenarios are reviewed. Within the therapeutic relationship, each repeated scene, and its affective element in particular, is acknowledged, borne, and put into perspective.

Gaining insight, learning from the past, putting emotional trauma into perspective, and arriving at new viewpoints—all converge on an aspect of treatment that attempts to provide patients with the tools of better living. From the two categories of "those who eat fish versus those who know how to fish," the goal of psychotherapy is to help patients achieve the greater self-sufficiency offered by the latter. Some psychiatrists (Binswanger, 1945; Progoff, 1973) have considered psychosis to be the organism's way of searching out much needed skills. Here the illness serves notice that the individual needs to strengthen or rearrange important parts of the psyche. How does health show itself? As affect is contained and works its way back into the fabric of the psyche, vitality reasserts itself. A change in clothes or, perhaps, more color may be the clue. The enlisting of new friends or reestablishing of old ties that elicit affection and hope may be seen. With disruptions and restorations of the therapeutic alliance and transference, unbearable affect can be reintegrated. The therapeutic relationship can become both a road map and a source of companionship as the patient heads forward into the future.

2

FORMS OF INTRODUCTION: THE CHIEF COMPLAINT

THE CHIEF COMPLAINT: AMY BETH MILLS

After a quick lunch with his best friend from college, Tony was musing on how he would institute this new policy—saying "no." Can you take on this patient? Could we meet to discuss this case? Would you organize the other residents for a journal club? After years of saying "yes," could he learn to say "no"?

The beeper startled him out of his contemplation. The only way to say "no" to that damn thing would be to turn it off. Then if one of the attendings tried to get in touch with you, there'd be real hell to pay. It was the psychiatry emergency room. Coming back to reality, he muttered "Oh, great," hustled out the locked door of the inpatient unit, down the stairs, and into the main lobby.

"Admission," Doris said. She barely looked up as she tossed the papers toward Tony.

"Is it bad?" he asked.

"How should I know?" she replied.

At least she looked up at him from her desk. Not that he particularly liked Doris, the outpatient secretary, but in some ways it was such a solitary job to be a psychiatry resident at Mount Sinai that even a little contact with the secretary was something.

15

He glanced over the papers as he strode down the hall to meet his patient:

> 31 y,o, SWF (single white female) with history of manic-depressive illness . . . brought in by older sister for walking out into street . . . stopping traffic . . . trying to proposition men driving cars . . . Stopped taking lithium and ?Navane?—

Tony couldn't quite make it out. Doctors have an impossible time reading other doctors' writing.

> . . . been having trouble with older sister for last two months since moved to area, worse yesterday, had a big argument . . .

His thought was that it was 4 P.M. and that it would be at least 6 before he could get out. He hated getting a late afternoon admission, everyone did. The irritation and bad mood, however, were completely blown away as he stepped into the interviewing room.

She turned so quickly from the window to the door that the initial visual image of her blurred. Her long sleek brown hair and her elegant pose looking out the window had barely enough time to register. Before he could begin his ritual "Hello, my name is Dr. Potter," she reeled around so fast that her sculpted high cheekbones, her classic nose, and startling blue eyes were within an inch of his face. Was she going to smash his face with hers or was she going to kiss him?

"Envy, you see, is like arsenic and old lace. It is a slow poison that creeps, in its petty pace from day to day to the last syllable of recorded time. It is a slow and ugly death of the spirit and flesh."

Just as quickly, she turned back to the window. Her timing, her articulation, and her delivery were artistic. In her opening lines, she hooked him. Potter was now captive audience to the life story and psychiatric treatment of Amy Beth Mills, the "manic-depressive psychotic."

So much for his new "say no" policy.   ✦

FIRST IMPRESSIONS

The chief complaint of a patient is like the title of a book, a play, or a song—it summarizes the content. Yet, the chief complaint does more. It also serves as an emotional introduction as well. Its introductory affective signature comprises both verbal and nonverbal components. The length, tense, sound, and parts of speech of the word (word morphology), how the words are arranged in the sentence (syntax), what the words mean (semantics), and how the words are presented as topics and in dialogue (pragmatics), along with the tone, inflection, and gesture of the voice and body (nonverbal components) all combine together in a unique affective way. Amy Mills serves up "envy" in the face of her new doctor. She delivers it in Shakespearean oratory. Her labeling envy as "poison" is confirmed by her description that it causes "a slow and ugly death."

Here is the emotional signature of the chief complaint. The word morphology breaks down into the use of many words with an "s" sound, such as "arsenic," "lace," "slow," "poison," and others. Alliteration and consonance are frequent. The syntax posits "envy" as a noun in a noun phrase in a series of noun phrases. The semantic components include, most importantly, envy as the "agent" of death. Other semantic attributes include envy having the characteristic of a slow poison, of being similar to arsenic. Its object is "spirit and flesh." The pragmatics of her communication include the paraphrase from Shakespeare, the brief soliloquy, the "in the face" posture, and the cadence of her speech.

Most chief complaints from psychotic patients are not as eloquent, complex, or dramatic as the one from Amy Mills. Yet, most do carry an initial affective signature. This is an essential aspect of the first communication. Often, a theme can be heard or a feeling-tone appreciated. The chief complaint is an affective announcement.

HOW EMOTION USES WORDS

In this exploration of the chief complaint, the spotlight is on the delivery of affect. A great observer of children and their intellectual development, Jean Piaget noticed that emotion and cognition were intimately related. Since Piaget (1959), clinicians and researchers have agreed that emotion and cognition are two sides of the same coin. Yet, the ways in which they bond together make for added value. Put under the research microscope, emotion can be seen to give form to cognition. And it comes out in words. Because words are pieces of the communication puzzle, it's important to be aware of how most of us structure them; then, we can better understand how psychotic patients rearrange words (Rosenbaum & Sonne, 1986).

We've seen how Amy Mills uses the first level of natural language processing to make her emotional mark. She uses word **morphology** in terms of sound, part of speech, assonance, and consonance to "hiss" her anger at Dr. Potter. She uses the second level of **syntax** to arrange the words within the sentence to convey the intensity of her anger. The insertion of the noun phrase "you see," ensnares the listener. The third level of **semantics** is particularly interesting. This level of natural language processing contains two structures. The linguists call these "case frames" and "object taxonomies" (Garfield & Rapp, 1992). Case frames define the roles that words play in a communication. Amy turns Envy into an "agent" whose "action" is to creep and to cause a consequence (death). An object taxonomy defines the properties and hierarchies of a word. Envy, like arsenic, in this communication, is a subset of the larger set of "poisons." Since poison does "spread" through the body, a listener might allow "creeping" as a substitution. Yet, "old lace" is not allowable semantically, as an equivalence for arsenic/poison. Artificial intelligence researchers have looked at psychotic speech and have noted the frequency of these kinds of semantic violations (Garfield & Rapp, 1994). Yet, notice what purpose these kinds of deviations produce. Amy Mills, in psychotic terms, but in no uncertain terms, has delivered her "feeling-toned" theme of anger and venom to Dr. Potter. Notice how the emotion structures the communication; here we see how emotion on the other side of the coin of cognition not only serves as part bonding agent but also "structures" the cognitions—in this case, the speech and language itself.

In Sullivan's (1953) interpersonal psychiatry, how the patient positions himself or herself is of key importance and, here, the fourth level of natural language processing, **pragmatics,** can be seen. The spotlight of emotion in Amy's sudden soliloquy shapes the gesture, pose, cadence, inflection, and rhythm of her chief complaint. Affect not only is conveyed by but actively structures these first introductions. Passion finds its voice in Amy Mills's chief complaint.

THE SPECIAL PLACE OF THE CHIEF COMPLAINT

Clinical medicine has always been attuned to the special significance of the patient's first words to the doctor. The art of understanding the patient—diagnosis—has, historically, stood on evidential foundations. Like Sherlock Holmes, physicians have adopted the role of detective and have sought to assemble pieces of evidence that will, ultimately, lead to a diagnosis. The editors (Thorn, Adams, Braunwald, Isselbacher, & Petersdorf, 1977) of *Harrison's Principles of Internal Medicine* remark in their introductory chapter:

> Ideally, the narration of symptoms should be in the patient's own words, the principal events being presented in the temporal order in which they occurred. . . . Something always is gained by listening to the patient and

noting the way in which he talks about his symptoms. Inflection of voice, facial expression and attitude may betray important clues as to the meaning of the symptoms to the patient. (p. 3)

We can see here that the general internist is being cued into the importance of the affective component of the chief complaint. The physician as expert observer, as a phenomenologist, is to pay special attention to nonverbal expressions of emotion as well as to the content of the presenting grievance itself.

A pioneering, midwestern psychiatrist, Karl Menninger (1952), in *A Manual for Psychiatric Case Study,* also emphasized that the "physician should cultivate an interest in everything about the patient. Detail often appears tedious and time consuming, but circumstantiality may be the best or only means available to the patient for communicating the significance of a particular event to him" (p. 28). Many authors (Bruch, 1974; Margulies & Havens, 1981; Roth, 1987) have focused on the elements of the initial interview, including how first impressions are formed and the importance of attending to the myriad factors that have contributed to the patient's seeking help. Interestingly, very few, if any have zeroed in on the patient's very first words, the chief complaint.

VERBAL AND NONVERBAL EMOTION IN THE CHIEF COMPLAINT

To discern the affect in the chief complaint, both verbal and nonverbal influences must be taken into account. The previously noted verbal components—morphology, syntax, semantics, and pragmatics—are particularly salient. Is the patient's first communication a statement? A question? Is it a rhetorical question or does it demand an answer? Amy Mills makes a statement. Whose turn is it?

The nonverbal components of emotion in the chief complaint are no less significant. Prosody—the conveyance of emotion in speech—must be discerned. Is she speaking in a monotonal voice? Speaking with intensity? To listen to Amy Mills is to hear a medium pitch, cadenced, melodic, yet, intense voice; a serious voice with a touch of venom. Anger, in multiple shadings, is delivered to the listener.

Electronics researchers call the "extraneous" noises—static, room sounds, time before first words—at the beginning of an audio or videotape the "windup signature." Each tape has a unique "fingerprint" in this way. Similarly, in the chief complaint in the psychiatric interview, the patient's linguistic and emotional (prosodic) components join together as a special "windup signature." Let's listen to another example from a different patient, Jack Barnes.

A 26-year-old Catholic man, Jack Barnes, was hospitalized after walking around an upscale part of Boston talking to parking meters. Jack has no friends and most of his contact is with his landlord, a 71-year-old man. Even then, Jack saw the landlord infrequently—only to pay rent. One night, toward the beginning of July, that time when new medical and psychiatric residents begin their training, Jack got drunk. He rarely drank. He then went around talking to parking meters until he was picked up by the police who, of course, took him to the hospital. He was assigned a new therapist.

Barnes: I guess I'm here again. (Spoken in a medium pitch, at a medium rate, with inflection on "I'm here," with eyes first glancing up at the start of the chief complaint and then looking downward at the end of the sentence with head posturing downward at the end of the sentence as well. His posture and tone conveyed feelings of embarrassment, sheepishness, and a slight degree of sadness.)

Dr. Potter responds to Jack's chief complaint:

Tony: When were you here before?

Barnes: Three years ago when I was shot in the arm in the army.

Tony: Ah . . .

Barnes: (noticing a plant in the office) Plants . . . uh, . . . hmmm . . .

Tony: Yes, plants—very true . . .

Barnes: Plants can be very dangerous—unless they are hanging higher than they can hurt you . . .

Tony: What could be more dangerous than a plant, hmmm?

Barnes: Cars—cars could be more dangerous than plants . . .

Tony: Yes, cars . . . potentially more dangerous . . . even more so than plants . . .

Barnes: (looking at therapist) Unless, of course you have a dangerous plant inside a harmless automobile. . . .

Aside from the captivating use of neologic to which Jack subscribes, a careful look at his chief complaint is revealing. He is sheepish, embarrassed, deferring, perhaps even a little bit ashamed to be back in the hospital again. Yet, there is more. His syntactic style is one wherein he offers up his words for mutual consideration. He makes a statement. Like most statements, it can be accepted, rejected, or modified. Although the content of the first exchange reveals concern about danger from sensitive life forms as well as commentary about the potential threat of powerful machines, the chief complaint is different. Notice his choice of words: "I **guess** I'm here again." Do you agree? What do you think about that? The affective tone of his chief complaint is one where he offers himself up for acceptance or rejection.

Later, the concern about danger emerges. This new focus on the chief complaint now includes the patient's pattern of "offering himself up" to those around him as well as the semantic concerns he expressed about danger. "Trusting too much" can be a cardinal sign of paranoid psychopathology (Garfield & Havens, 1991). One can wonder about the earlier patterns of offering that the patient engaged in and how those offers were received and treated. The old psychiatric records, as they often do, filled in much of the missing story, how Jack continually offered himself up to please his alcoholic father. Yet, the old man was never there for him; dad was out drinking and was present only in a fleeting, erratic, and tenuous way.

Although his chief complaint was a complete sentence, most of his communications were not. In fact, Jack rarely completes a full sentence and rarely strings one full sentence to another. This aspect of the pragmatics of his speech was true also of how he kept appointments. He never came on time or left on time—he was either late or lingered on in the sessions. He might be found in a nearby hallway at the time of the appointment. This tentativeness continued the emotional tone of his chief complaint.

THE CHIEF COMPLAINT PROPER

The patient's articulation of what it is that brings him to the doctor is contiguous but somewhat different from the patient's first uttered words. How the patient introduces himself, actually meets the doctor, is the initial part of the chief complaint. What might be termed the "chief complaint proper" would be the patient's description of the presenting problem—how he understands what it is that is bothering him. This problem description, whether it be depression or ants controlling one's bodily sensation via their antennae, is also an emotional communication. Of more importance is how the emotion of the chief complaint proper **confirms** or **disconfirms** the affect conveyed by the verbal and nonverbal components of the first words (or sounds). Amy Mills's first words are also her chief complaint proper; whereas for Jack Barnes, his first communications did not convey a description of how he understood why he was in the hospital.

A key element to discerning the affect lodged in the description of the problem—the chief complaint proper—is the clinician's empathic abilities. The ability to place oneself in the patient's shoes and to attempt to feel what he or she must be feeling is the essence of this very important process.

A NOTE OF CAUTION

How does the impression of the doctor affect the patient's first productions? Do different words come out depending on the doctor-stranger whom the patient meets? Harry Stack Sullivan (1954) was known for his exquisite talent in talking to psychotic patients; he emphasized that interpersonal forces influence both communication and symptomatology. He first confirmed the importance of the emotional aspect of the chief complaint: "The psychiatrist should also have learned what sorts of immediate impressions he himself obtains from the appearance and initial movements and vocal behavior of another" (p. 14). He also cautioned: "The psychiatrist must be alert to learn, insofar as possible, the immediate impression of him which is created in a stranger" (pp. 69–70). Margulies and Havens (1981) expanded on this phenomenon of the presence of the doctor shaping what comes out of the patient's mouth by adding:

> Essentially, what the patient presents is in part determined by our impact on him. We must therefore be alert to the kinds of anticipations and projections this provokes in the patient. Furthermore, the patient's presentation of himself can be expected to have a characteristic impact on us. (p. 424)

For Amy mills, one might argue that she was not influenced in the least by whether the psychiatric resident was male or female because she turned so swiftly from the window to the doctor that she wouldn't have had time to select her presentation. It would be argued that she had composed her chief complaint prior to his appearance. Yet, had she been told to whom she had been assigned prior to Dr. Potter's arrival? Did she know it was a man? Could she see his reflection in the window? In short, even in this seemingly clear-cut case, the clinician cannot be certain how his or her presence may have altered the patient's announcement.

WORKING WITH THE OPENING REMARKS: EXTRACTING AFFECT

Are the first words uttered the chief complaint? Is that what the clinician should focus on first? No, the first words are not necessarily the **content** of the chief complaint, but yes, the emotional communication of the first words uttered does require attention. These first words, along with the patient's "body language," will speak volumes about the patient's overall mood and affect.

For example, let's say that the patient is a 40-year-old white man who is sent by his mother for consultation because she believes he is paranoid; he believes that he is unhappy. The clinician opens the door to the waiting room and notices how he immediately pops up and says "Hi. I'm Marcus." He is smiling, he offers his hand and says "Marcus Reed." After a survey of Mr. Reed's clothes, the therapist notes his light orange t-shirt neatly tucked into clean gray slacks; the patient also has on basketball sneakers. He is also carrying a clipboard. The nonverbal emotional components of Mr. Reed's first presentation include his attire, posture, movement, facial expression, and the tone of his voice. His words are "Hi. I'm Marcus." A greeting. He names himself and he identifies himself. From these spoken and unspoken affective cues, the clinician might conclude that this guy is friendly, casual, wants to write things down, and is not particularly suspicious. He is not sheepish, embarrassed, or deferential like Jack Barnes. He does not serve up "envy" in the therapist's face like Amy Mills. Marcus is coming to meet his new therapist—he conveys an emotional tone of trustworthiness and appeal. He wants to please. He's eager, he's optimistic. The emotion that wraps together the verbal and the nonverbal is that of "hope."

It might be argued that within the disparate elements of the first encounter many emotions are vying for attention. The task, therefore, is to allow these disparate affective impressions to be received and recorded in toto and then to "wrap" them together under a dominant affective category. This is the essence of a first emotional gestalt.

Armed with the knowledge of the emotional woof of Mr. Reed's presentation, the therapist can now move on to specifically identify the chief complaint proper, the content of Mr. Reed's complaint. What will Marcus state as his problem? He comes in, he's tentative but friendly. He says he's not sure why he's there but there's a conflict between him and his mother. There are people who, for whatever reason, are sabotaging his work. He's an engineering student. At this point, the therapist would want to clarify that there's a conflict and that the patient feels sabotaged. He agrees. Through a process of clarification, the clinician and patient settle on an understanding of what bothers him. Here is the content of the chief complaint. Where is the emotion here?

As a clinician, the task at this point is to call on an empathic position to glean the affect in the content of the chief complaint proper. So, first it is essential to take in the emotional elements, then one clarifies the trouble, and next, one uses introspection to arrive at an emotional understanding of what things must be like for the patient. What must it feel like to be in the midst of a conflict with someone so important and, at the same time, to experience yourself as sabotaged? It must be disheartening to be Marcus Reed. Thus, the clinician must, transiently, try to be the patient. From the person (mother) you **hoped** would be one of your strongest allies, you receive a profound lack of support—in fact, she is in opposition to you. She stands in the way of your hopes. You are in need of hope. Perhaps, not hopeless but in less hope. Thus, as a clinician, one receives confirmation from the content of the problem of the emotional gestalt that has already been gleaned from the verbal and nonverbal tone of the first words uttered. The feeling tone of the "feeling-toned complex" is that of hope versus a lot less hope.

For the sake of comparison, let's go back and reconstruct the initial contact with Marcus Reed, changing either the verbal or nonverbal component of the first words and let's examine the impact on the affective signature that the new "Marcus Reed" would write upon us. Let's say that the clinician opens the door to the waiting room and Marcus is sitting on the waiting room couch and he does not look up. The therapist says "Marcus Reed?" with an inquiring tone. Mr. Reed snorts a short exhale of breath from his nose while still looking down and then turns his head to look at the therapist. His mouth is in a grimace/smile, his nostrils are widened, and his nose moves up as though he is smelling something with a bad odor. The clinician might say "Hi. I'm Doctor Potter," and the patient stands up but does not move toward the clinician or away from him. Let's say that the clinician takes a step back, opens the door a little wider, and says "Won't you come in?" The therapist turns and walks to his chair in the office and Mr. Reed walks in slowly, looking around at the pictures, books, desks, and so forth. He is wearing a light orange t-shirt neatly tucked into clean gray slacks and has on basketball sneakers.

How are you to determine the emotion in this introduction? Basically, the first sounds the patient makes are not words, but instead are sounds, in fact, a snort. Is he a pig? Disgruntled? Disgusted? Contemptuous? He does not stand up to greet the therapist but rather turns his head. Is he tired or is it that he can't be bothered? Is it all much too much of an effort? There is the attempt at a smile but the grimace overtakes it. Is his silence due to embarrassment or sadness or to not wanting to make the effort? His gait and movement in investigating the office may reflect an uneasiness with the new environment and a systematic evaluation of the clinician on the basis of the office fixtures. The emotional gestalt of the first words/sounds—the snort—is at one with the nonverbal communication of an affect of disdain or contempt. This is an example of how the therapist should look for confirmation or nonconfirmation amongst the elements of nonverbal emotion in the chief complaint. Is this Marcus Reed **disgusted** with this entire enterprise? Let's see what he says as the doctor and patient begin to clarify the chief complaint proper.

Let's say that the therapist tells Mr. Reed that his understanding of why Mr. Reed is here is that his mother thinks he is "paranoid," whatever that means, and that he, Marcus Reed himself, is unhappy. He might now correct the therapist and say that "no," he is not unhappy but rather, he is hassled. His mother is not a problem except that he has to live at her house for the time being and she annoys him with her questions. What really is bothering him is that people are sabotaging his work. They know that he has new and, potentially, very marketable ideas about an engineering project and they are trying to mess it up. If they could, they would steal the project themselves but he has established protections against that happening.

So, first, the clinician has established an emotional gestalt of "contempt or disgust," and then the clinician attempts to clarify the problem. Allowing the patient space to correct the understanding is essential because to be empathic, the therapist must know the patient's attitude. A full understanding must be in place. At this point, the clinician might clarify the chief complaint proper and say that his understanding is that Mr. Reed is under attack because he is the object of envy. He concurs. Now, to pull out the affect, the therapist must next move to the empathic position. How must it **feel** to be thwarted in one's endeavors because one is envied by others? It would make anybody angry. But is there more? How does it feel being thwarted **because** one is so good? Perhaps, "indignation" would be the emotion. As a general guideline, the therapist must spend a lot of time and attention on this step of initial empathic affective attunement. And in this second Marcus Reed example, is there possibly still more? One is thwarted and attacked **by those** who are **less** creative: Is "pity" the emotional result? Perhaps, it would be a feeling of pity if they weren't constantly an "annoyance." How do pity and annoyance fuse together? The empathic process allows for the amalgam emotion to emerge: "Contempt," "disdain," or "disgust" are the main probabilities. Once again, there is that all-important resonance between form and content, between the verbal and nonverbal forms of emotion; between the various levels of communication. The feeling-toned complex of our Marcus Reed, number two, is one of disgust.

WHY THE EMOTIONAL FIRST IMPRESSION IS CLINICALLY IMPORTANT

The gestalt of the first emotional imprint of the patient is important because it sets the stage for how the first interaction and, in fact, the course of the whole treatment itself is constructed. For Marcus Reed number one, we must attend to his hope. For Marcus Reed number two, we must attend to his disgust. The two stories for Marcus Reed are the same until each individual one is first met. Of course, the first encounter is often over the telephone, but the first affective imprint is often not until the two strangers meet. Yet, for both patients, now so clearly different, a different story will emerge. The clinician will need to attend to the history of diminished hopes in Marcus Reed number one, and to the history of the development of disgust in the other. What events both recently and in the past set this dominant emotional tone in play?

THE ISSUE OF AFFECT INTENSITY

A final thread in gleaning the affect of the first encounter is found in discerning of the intensity of affect. Amy Mills conveys a "very intense" feeling by the **speed** of her movement, by the **proximity** of her body to Dr. Potter (she moves in extremely close) and in the loudness of her voice. The emotional tone presents itself with great intensity. The same can be said for Marcus Reed number two. His speed is extremely slow, his sounds are extremely few, his distance is extremely great, and his gaze is extremely wide in range. Each component of the verbal and non-verbal emotion has a range and frequency. The facial expression of disgust is intense. His nose lifts up **a lot** indicating that the odor is "very" bad. His disdain/disgust is again intensely conveyed in his description of his mother being insignificant and a minor "annoyance." Different words within an emotion category will be selected to indicate intensity; for example, the term "conflict" is less intense than the word "war." And the word war is less intense than the phrase "a duel to the death." Thus, Marcus Reed, number one, has a **moderately** intense feeling tone.

The intensity of his hope does not induce him to pump your hand up and down many times (great frequency). It does not configure the length of his sentence to be "Gee, am I glad to finally meet you" (syntax). It is not that intense. He is not without any hope.

Clinicians need to know about affect intensity as well as dominant affect category because much of what the psychotherapy of psychosis is about is the modulation and integration of affect. The goal here is not to make dispassionate those who are inflamed but, rather, to keep them from burning up. Knowing how intense the hope, envy, fear, or disgust is can help the clinician figure out what is necessary to permit an alliance to take shape. How deep does it go? Here is the psychotherapist as navigator. Do these initial affective communications bespeak many dark stormy clouds or is there a thin sliver of red on the horizon (sailor's delight)? Are the waves too high? Close observation of affect intensity is essential to charting the course.

SUMMARY—AFFECT AND INTRODUCTION

To summarize the steps in extracting emotion from the chief complaint, clinicians must first be aware that the emotional gestalt will be formed by verbal and nonverbal elements within the initial introduction. Therapists must pay attention to the sounds made, the sounds of the specific words uttered, the arrangement of the words as spoken, and the style of turn-taking in the initial communication. Therapists must also pay attention to nonverbal components such as grooming, style and color of dress, gait, gesture, and manner—all which will convey an emotional tone. Next, it is important to note how these verbal and nonverbal cues are in or out of synch with each other. Then, clinicians must listen to the chief complaint proper and carefully clarify the patient's problem. Once the patient's position and attitude toward his or her problem have been determined, clinicians must go through an internal empathic attunement process to arrive at how they would feel given these circumstances presented by the patient. Again, this emotion should confirm what has been gleaned from the emotion extracted from the patient's first utterances and mannerisms. Finally, clinicians can arrive at a best guess of what unbearable affect afflicts the patient.

With this knowledge of emotion in the first encounter and its various components, keep in mind this note of caution expressed earlier: The clinician may be a thorn in the patient's foot or salve in the patient's wound, even from the very start. And, along with the power of observation, the clinician may have other tools (Havens, 1986) for "sounding the depth" of the patient's immediate affective state. Important questions remain. Does the extent of past psychological trauma result in a greater degree of feeling-toned intensity? Sometimes it does. Affect may need to be defused in order to establish a treatment platform. Too intense a disgust or anger may make the office impossible as a safe place for treatment to take place. Marcus Reed number two is disgusted by being the object of envy, whereas Amy Mills is angry about envy. Where do we turn to understand the difference? With these questions in mind, we now turn to the issue of emotion in the precipitating event.

3

PSYCHOTIC THEMES IN THE PRECIPITATING EVENT

THE PRECIPITATING EVENT: AMY BETH MILLS REVISITED

A few hours before the police took her to Boston's Mount Sinai Hospital, Amy Mills had been fixing breakfast in her sister's apartment in Coolidge Corner. Actually, since Amy was paying half the rent, it was technically, hers and Ellen's apartment; Ellen, however, was extraordinarily picky about what Amy could or could not do in it. Their little brother John's graduation ceremony from Wesleyan College had been difficult for the two of them. Amy felt that Ellen was constantly trying to "put on airs" with John's fraternity friends, and when Amy did a little flirting of her own, Ellen kept telling their father that Amy was getting "psychotic" again.

In an effort to keep the peace, Amy slowly sliced an orange into quarters and offered the small plateful to Ellen. The two girls had always liked fresh fruit.

"Ugh. Get this out of my face," Ellen said in disgust and then smiled a fake smile and said, "please."

"Whatever . . ." Amy pulled the dish away so quickly that two quarters of the orange fell to the floor. She carried the plate back to the sink from the kitchen table.

"Could you please not get sticky juice all over my clean kitchen floor, Amy?" Ellen chided.

"It's not sticky and it's not . . ." As Amy began her protest, Ellen interrupted:

"I suppose I'll have to clean up the mess, right?"

Amy had just about had it. . . . Why don't you run in traffic? Go play in traffic, bitch. Go play in traffic, honey. In traffic. . . . The words came louder in her head.

"Are you going to clean it up, Amy? Come on, I've got to get to work." Ellen pushed her chair back from the table.

Amy ran out of the room and threw open the front door. Still in her flower print nightrobe, she ran toward Beacon Street. When cars stopped at the light, Amy looked in. If there was a guy driving the car, she pressed her lips against the glass of his window and waved. "I can play this game," she thought to herself. "In traffic, in traffic," the voices said. "I can play this game in traffic," she said to herself.

The cars started honking and a few had to swerve to avoid her. Ellen had come after her. The newspaper shop owner had called the police. They took Amy to Mount Sinai Hospital's psychiatric emergency room where she gazed out the window of the examining room while she waited for the doctor.   ✦

AFFECT IN THE PRECIPITATING EVENT

Amy had been sick before. Every time she started to get her life back together, something happened. This time it was an unfortunate exchange with her sister. Affect reaches its first breaking point in the original precipitating event.

In the previous chapter, the bond between Andrew Stevens and his father can no longer contain the despair the young man feels at the loss of hope for a life and love of his own. Subsequent events, with similar themes are like the proverbial straws that break the camel's back. For Andrew Stevens, the "straw" might be a boss's disapproval of an important suggestion made by Andrew or Andrew's not being promoted. For Amy Mills, the sticking point is in her sister's putting her down.

There is an important time in the course of the patient's life when things take a turn for the worse. Somehow, the internal gyroscope that more or less keeps the patient's travels on line gets knocked off balance. Either through internal or external cues, the patient discovers that his or her life is no longer on course. It is a painful discovery, causing a host of distressing feelings and meanings to the patient.

Often, after the first break, the patient no longer feels like his or her "old self." In the recovery or adjustment period, specific experiences may turn the tide back toward psychosis. In looking back to those times, through careful inquiry, the clinician can find the outline of a specific scenario in the patient's mind, marking that recent point at which life has changed for the worse. That scenario—the "straw that broke the camel's back," is what we call "the precipitating event." Unbearable affect reaches its peak in the precipitating event.

THE HISTORY OF THE PRECIPITATING EVENT

Breuer and Freud (1893/1981), in their landmark "Preliminary Communication," outlined one of the first major theories concerning early psychic trauma, psychic causality, precipitating event, and psychopathology:

> A chance observation has led us, over a number of years, to investigate a great variety of different forms and symptoms of hysteria, with a view to discovering their precipitating cause—the event which provoked the first occurrence, often many years earlier, of the phenomena in question. (p. 3)

They postulated that psychopathology resulted from an intolerable early life trauma. The intolerable original trauma is repressed and banished from consciousness. The original event arises again, in disguised form, through hysterical symptomatology. Psychotherapy, then, works its curative effects by bringing the trauma into consciousness and discharging it through affect, words, or corrective associations.

The "Preliminary Communication" concentrated primarily on the original childhood trauma, not on the scenario prior to the onset of illness. They felt the later scenario was "trivial" and simply "re-minded" the patient of the earlier stress. Thus, Freud and Breuer did not attempt to explain the scenario in which the straw was added and the camel's back broken but rather, postulated an explanation of why the camel developed a bad back. Freud and Breuer would probably not have focused on the interaction between Amy and Ellen and Amy's subsequent kissing of men through car windows; instead, they would have delved into the early events and relationships that might have led to Amy's psychotic vulnerabilities.

Ellenberger (1970), a prolific psychoanalytic historian, has pointed out that the "Preliminary Communication" had, as its antecedents, both Pierre Janet's concept of "subconscious fixed ideas" and Benedikt's notion of the "pathogenic secret." At the turn of the century, Janet studied a multitude of symptoms of both psychotic and hysterical patients at the famous Salpetriere Hospital in Paris. Working in Charcot's laboratory, Janet used hypnosis and, later, narcoanalysis to elucidate his concept of the "subconscious fixed idea." Benedikt believed that ideas, like germs, could fester in the psyche and cause great disturbance. Freud, then, adopted many of Janet's ideas. According to Freud and Breuer, a kind of hidden, virulent idea was lodged in the patient's mind. In fact, in his early work, Freud would press on the patient's forehead in an attempt to jar free the pathogenic idea.

Adolph Meyer came from the same European training tradition as Freud and followed a similar path from neurology to psychology, yet Meyer (1951) took a slightly different tack toward the precipitating event. In keeping close to clinical observations of the patient, Meyer stressed the necessity of the clinician's having a detailed knowledge of the "situation" of the patient's life in chronological order. In Meyerian investigation, the details of the precipitating event are central; they serve not as a trivial reminding of the patient, but rather, as a situation that carries a burden to the patient that cannot be coped with by the patient's usual methods. Meyer emphasizes that symptomatology is actually the patient's way of "adjusting" or coping with unbearable burdens. Here is the classical notion of defensive efforts of the patient equating to psychotic symptomatology. This notion of psychosis as psychic conflict with primitive defenses was rearticulated in 1969 by Jacob Arlow and Charles Brenner (Arlow & Brenner, 1969), two prominent New York psychoanalysts.

The precipitating event, like the chief complaint, contains much thematic information that can be of use to the psychiatric clinician. Dr. Potter needs to know: Who is envious of whom or what? Is the envy inside Amy or does it surround her? Are these verbal exchanges between Amy and Ellen straws of envy that are too much for the patient to bear? What unbearable affect does this envy evoke inside Amy? Freud and Breuer look to the camel's back, but first, like Adolph Meyer, the clinician must seek to understand the nature of the straws that break that back. To help a patient rechart his or her life's course, one must determine the direction that life had been going prior to the onset or exacerbation of the illness. What were Amy Mills's most recent aspirations? Here, the clinician needs to know about the patient's condition just prior to the precipitating event and gain a thorough understanding of the event itself.

UNLOCKING THE PRECIPITATING EVENT: BURKE'S PENTAD

Kenneth Burke, a literary critic, was an astute observer of the human condition. In his *A Grammar of Motives* (1969), Burke provides a framework that can be quite useful for clinicians wishing to understand the precipitating event. In exploring the elements that are common to all human motives, he identifies the pentad of essentials in the motivation behind any event:

> We shall use five terms as the generating principle of our investigation. They are: Act, Scene, Agent, Agency, Purpose. In a rounded statement about motives, you must have some word that names the "act" (names what took place, in thought or deed), and another that names the "scene" (the background of the act, the situation in which it occurred); also, you must indicate what person or kind of person ("agent") performed that act, what means or instruments he used ("agency"), and the "purpose."

Burke's classification can be of assistance to both patient and clinician as they attempt to understand what has thrown the patient's life off course. By identifying the affective theme lodged in the precipitating event, one can extrapolate possible future scenarios that might also disrupt the patient's equilibrium. Anticipating circumstances that will arouse unbearable affect may help patients avoid those situations and can make life somewhat less threatening.

When the scenario that dislodged the patient's usual self is isolated, Burke's categories can provide a very useful analytic framework. Like the news reporter, the clinician is interested in who, what, why, where, when, and how. It is important to note that by attempting to categorize the act that took place, or the specifics of the scene, the clinician is not at all guaranteed real **certainty.** On the contrary, one must actually **plan** that significant ambiguity will be present in the report. However, this does not detract from the importance or utility of establishing the specifics within the five categories. Although "why" the event took place may not be as the patient reports, it is important to note it, because, in the patient's mind, a purpose is inferred. And the same is true for "how" what occurred did occur—it is not veracity that the clinician is interested in; rather, for the patient, there are, at the time, "agents" and "instruments" by which the purpose was accomplished. In cataloging the precipitating event into Burke's pentad of ingredients, landmarks are established that can serve as strategic points for clinical departure.

A close look at Dr. Potter's work with Amy Mills demonstrates the utility of Burke's framework. Although not detailed earlier, Amy pulled the reference to traffic from her mother, who always yelled at her to stay out of traffic; thus, Dr. Potter can understand the setting of Amy's acute decompensation. The action component of Burke's pentad of elements has to do with "kissing." In getting to know Amy's history, Dr. Potter learned that the "kissing of boys" action may have had its origins in

Ellen's adolescent promiscuousness. Ellen would boast to Amy about "making out" with high school boys. Of course, the recent flirting at their brother's graduation ties into the kissing of men act. In an interesting way, auditory hallucinations can be viewed as agents in Burke's framework. For Amy, the voice saying "honey" probably came from a college roommate who always called her honey. Later, this "sweet" roommate betrayed Amy. Dr. Potter could understand the purpose or "why" of this scene with its theme of betrayal. In the exchange over the oranges, Amy feels put down and betrayed by Ellen. Using Burke's strategic points of investigation leads to a deeper understanding of the straw that now breaks Amy's back.

MODES OF INTERPRETATION

An interesting and unforeseen benefit of using Burke's framework in assessing the precipitating event is that it provides a kind of metaframework for utilizing a variety of interpretive modes. The neo-Jungian analyst, Progoff (1973), identified three main interpretive modes in clinical psychiatry: (1) The principle of causality (Freud and Breuer's early postulations stand out here), that what is happening now is a "result" of what has happened before; (2) the principle of teleology (the existential and Adlerian schools of psychoanalysis stand out here), that what is happening now is part of the search for meaning in attaining one's "hopes" and "ideals"; and (3) the principle of synchronicity (Jung and Progoff come to the foreground here), that what is happening now may have no reason or purpose but is meaningfully coincidental and coherently related to certain other events also happening now. The pentad of ingredients that Burke outlines allows for the application of any of these three perspectives in the clinical understanding of the precipitating event. In this way, this kind of attention affords both clinician and theoretician a new testing ground for theory and practice building and rebuilding.

The three principles of interpretation—causal, teleologic, and synchronistic—have their correlates in the temporal dimensions of past, future, and present. Clearly, events occur in each dimension. Clinicians can take the elements of event and evaluate the patient's life course from each principle of interpretation using the precipitating event as the starting point. Whether Dr. Potter deals with Amy Mills's current life, her past life, or her feelings about her new doctor and her hopes for the future, the precipitating event to her present illness contains all the necessary ingredients. Dr. Potter might choose to focus on the historical threads of Amy's relationship with Ellen and their mother in looking at the kissing action and the traffic setting. Or, he might, instead, focus in on the current synchronistic intersection of Ellen and Amy's lives as Ellen tries to have a relationship with a man while Amy tries to gain a footing in day-to-day life. Here Burke's props might be the men in cars. Finally, Dr. Potter might focus on the future hopes of Amy, who desperately is looking for some kind of safe place where her own voice might be heard. This is the agent of hallucinations in Burke's format as well as the why of the scene—a response to betrayal.

AFFECT AND INVESTIGATION

After the introductions are over, what does the therapist do when dealing with a new patient? The chief complaint, one way or another has been presented. Is it now time for an exploration of the problem and the past? The clinician may ask: "What happened to bring you here?" Or is the better approach to look toward the future? The therapist might inquire: "What would you like to have happen here?" A final alternative would be to keep things in the here and now. "Here we are," the clinician might declare. In the discussion that follows on the heels of the chief complaint, a variety of affective notes will be sounded. Whichever approach the therapist takes, usually some kind of description of past problem, present dilemma, or future desire will emerge. It is said that affect is lodged in detail. Unbearable affect is lodged in the precipitating event—the past, present, and future all revolve around this unbearable emotion.

The case of Peter Laurence is an example. Lean, tall, and pleasant, this 23-year-old man wheels himself into the examining room in the emergency room of the hospital where the doctor has come to see him. Mr. Laurence had already announced that he was being healed by divine powers. The thought swirls about in the clinician's mind: Is his faith somehow related to his being wheelchair bound? This patient is a believer—he has hope. Now what?

In the room, the doctor follows the patient's lead and comments that his understanding is that Mr. Laurence is being healed by divine powers. The clinician might tell the patient that it is a curious thing that a man with such divine luck has been so unlucky to have been taken to a psyche emergency room. The patient replies: "I snapped." At this reference to a past event, one can almost hear the sound of something snapping. "Oh my God!" the clinician might exclaim, startled by the sudden, sharp break. An empathic attunement is in place. The therapist can feel the snap. Something of this magnitude, no doubt, calls for suprahuman intervention. "What happened?" the doctor inquires.

Peter goes on to describe the scene of the "snap." He had been working for a state legislator. His job had been to write position papers for the budget changes that the congressman wanted to introduce. Peter had also agreed to help his boss with the congressman's reelection campaign. They were traveling to a rally in one of the state cars. One of the congressman's aides, Linda, helped him into the middle front seat of the sedan and she put his wheelchair in the trunk. He had polio when he was a boy leaving him unable to walk without help. His boss drove and Linda sat on his right—also in the front seat. It was kind of cramped. Linda and his boss were actively discussing some campaign issue about which Peter knew little. He kept quiet. He knew the boss was attracted to Linda; she was 25 years old, brunette, pretty, and lively. They talked "over him" for quite some time. At some point in the ride, something inside him "snapped." "I knew then that I would be healed, my polio would be healed by the divine power of Jesus Christ." He added that once at the rally, he knew he was being healed and refused to use the wheelchair, even though getting around was difficult. They eventually convinced him to come to the hospital.

Even though Burke's five categories may seem somewhat abstract at first, they can provide a concrete means of understanding what is happening with Peter. The therapist can quickly spot the agents or actors. They consist of the boss, Peter, and the pretty girl. Identifying the action is next. The pretty girl and the boss are "talking over" Peter. The doctor can identify the props—the front seat of a sedan; words in motion. What about the setting?

"Did you snap at the **end of the ride** as you got to the rally or before that?" the doctor asks. It was a short while before that, he answers. "Were you thinking or looking out the window or . . ." the clinician questions. "I wasn't thinking about anything in particular . . . I was just looking out the window." Pressing for the "setting" even more, the clinician might ask: "Did you notice anything in particular?" Peter replies: "No. Just the road . . . a football field." A football field.

The doctor decides to ask Peter if he played football prior to his contracting polio or if he was friends with football players or went to football games when he was younger. These are important associations to the setting of "snapped." This is exactly what Jung (1907/1976) was referring to when he described the feeling-toned complex as being like a molecule with many atoms connecting onto it. Peter winced when asked about playing football, and somewhat cynically offered that this was a college football field and he hadn't tried out for the team. In this exploration of the precipitating event, the clinician now discovers the emotion of bitterness—had something left a bad taste in Peter's mouth? Is bitterness the feeling-tone glue that holds all the associations together?

"How did you know it was a college football field?" Here, the doctor asks more about the scene of the current snap. Peter looks at the clinician as though the clinician was incredibly dumb and replies that he went to college at Parkside, the same place. He knew the college well. At this point in the interview, he looks off to the side and starts to talk. He comments that, he had, in fact, spent time at this football field during college. He had a crush on a young woman, Claire, who took him to several games in the fall of his junior year. She had dated a fellow, on and off, who played on the squad and who was quite accepting of Peter's being wheelchair bound and of him. Peter liked this guy. Secretly, Peter loved Claire and wondered/hoped that she might love him too. They went to one game where Parkside won the game. Afterward, the two of them ran into her old boyfriend. Claire and the football player argued at length while Peter sat passively by in his wheelchair. He realized at that moment that it was the football player that Claire felt passionately about, not him.

The feeling tone of the precipitating event led into a past event that was pivotal for the patient. This is often what happens during the process of affect diagnosis. The deeper layers are connected by their common feeling tone. The affective theme of despair and hopelessness at being the "third wheel" makes itself palpably known in the exploration of the scene of the "snap." The doctor might conclude that the earlier trauma from college is now "displaced" onto the action, actors, and scene in the current congressman/aide scenario. Here, despair is the core emotion lodged in the precipitating event. Peter's delusion of being healed by Jesus Christ revolves around this feeling-toned complex of not being able to secure that which might allow him to feel whole—the love of a cherished woman. How had his early experience with polio influenced his self-image? What role did the love of this woman play in that self-image? These are crucial issues for the treatment that now are able to be seen.

Another example may illuminate how important it is for therapists to gain a complete understanding of the components of the precipitating event. This is the case of a 66-year-old retired, quiet gray-haired Catholic woman who had worked most of her life in the post office. Edna Tomason is her name and she greets the therapist with a weak smile. She manages to eke out a hello and halfhearted handshake. She says that she can't get over some depression she's been having. She seems defeated.

She begins slowly, without any need for prompting, to tell her story. She lost her husband some 13 years ago. He died after a coronary bypass operation. After that, she was on her own for 3 years, still working at the post office, and then she met an elderly gentleman, Ben, with whom she developed a close friendship. Although he eventually moved into her house, they decided not to marry. Like her first husband, Ben also suffered from angina and from gastric ulcers as well. He was not physically active like her husband had been, but Edna found him to be a loyal and attentive companion.

The trouble was with her neighbor, Clarence Mann. He, too, was 66 years old and his house on the corner had been "grandfathered" into the town's zoning laws to be a crafts gallery on the first floor. His residence was on the second floor. Unfortunately, she added, her house and Mr. Mann's house shared a common access road that was, technically, almost all on his property. Furthermore, Mr. Mann had an "obnoxious" streak in him such that he would "leer" sexually at Edna and tell her that she was wasting precious years and fine assets on the ailing Ben. Clarence was a handsome man, but she found his remarks very insulting and not flattering. Generally, she ignored them.

About 6 months ago, Mr. Mann set up a roadside display and sales stand at the very front of his property. As a consequence, the traffic in front of Edna's house increased dramatically. Although she and Ben didn't like it (she now looks up at the therapist), they could live with it. But 4 weeks ago, while going out front to pick up her newspaper, what does she see? Workmen were installing a cement partition along Mr. Mann's length of the access road. She realized that she would have no way to turn her car around in the common driveway and she would have to back her car out directly into the busy street. When she confronted Clarence about the position this put her in, he bluntly told her that it wasn't his problem and he wasn't going to change his mind. Then the depression set in.

The elements of the precipitating event, as assessed by the therapist, are as follows: the setting was the outside of the house—driveway, yard, neighbor's yard, and street. The actors were elderly men—one of whom was handsome, one of whom was ailing—and an attractive older woman. The prop was the concrete partition. The action was her being "cut off." As for the purpose, it was to benefit the handsome man at her expense. With these elements in hand, the clinician, again, uses introspection and empathy to put himself in her shoes. At first pass, the affective theme that emerges is one of being cut off by a man, which results in being put in a dangerous situation. Betrayal and fear come to the foreground.

Keeping the Burkean components of the precipitating event in mind, the therapist later finds out that when Edna was a young girl, around 4 years old, her father suddenly left the house. Her dad had been a charismatic and handsome fellow, and he abandoned Edna and her mother. She and her mother struggled financially for some time thereafter. It is not uncommon for therapists who focus on affect and the precipitating event to have what has been called the "ah ha!" experience when finding out about the patient's past. With Edna Tomason, this information about her father is confirmation of the feeling-toned complex at work. First, betrayal and fear are announced by the chief complaint, then located in the precipitating event, and later confirmed by the developmental history. The therapist can feel himself on the "affective road map of the past" as emotions are displaced first to her husband, and then split between Ben and Clarence. What new worries will isolation from a charismatic man bring? What if Ben has a heart attack? Will she be able to get him to the hospital in time if she can't get her car turned around? The therapist is moved by her distress; it is graphic.

TOOLS OF THE TRADE—SUMMARY OF THE PRECIPITATING EVENT

Notions of psychic conflict and deficit are not quite enough to make the clinician's way in working with psychosis. Knowing that there is or are intolerable emotions is a start. Listening and attending to the elements of the chief complaint for its affective imprimatur can help set the stage for an initial appreciation of the quality and depth of the feeling tone. Unlocking the precipitating event into setting, action, actors, props, and purposes is a next helpful tool. Unbearable affect swirls within the precipitating event. It is important for a thorough exploration of the event that occurred prior to presentation to take place. Here, the clinician may be unsure whether to focus on what the patient thinks happened prior to presentation or on what third parties report. A good rule of thumb is to collect both reports in case they are not the same. An empathic appraisal of both scenarios will give the best chance of extracting what affect is intolerable to the patient. Frequently, the patient cannot bear the resulting emotion and may block out the event. The third-party report of what happened then becomes essential. But if the patient does report a scenario that is markedly different, it is also essential for the clinician to attend to it. Within the patient's mind, something has happened, and it has led to the patient feeling a certain way. The clinician must appreciate the patient's feeling state. Armed with the patient's affective signature from the chief complaint and new emotional knowledge from the precipitating event, the clinician can arrive at a judgment of what unbearable emotions now move the patient. To have a better grasp of how emotion has its way in psychosis, one must also look behind the patient's presentation and observe the mind's machinery at work.

4

AFFECT AND PRIMARY PROCESS IN PSYCHOSIS

THE PRIMARY PROCESS: AMY AND NANCY

D r. Tony Potter wondered whether he could make a go of becoming a psychotherapist. It wasn't so much a philosophical question as it was a pragmatic one. At times, it seemed easier to understand the musing of his psychotic patients than it was to understand the healthier ones. One of his teachers had commented that people took "normality" for granted and worried a great deal about pathology when, in fact—given the billions of decisions the human organism had to make from applying the right amount of pressure to the toothpaste tube and activating the proper finger musculature to, God forbid, driving a car—it was amazing anyone dared get up in the morning. A psychotic break, in this light, did not seem like such a big deal, nor an unlikely event. The waiter asked him for the second time what he would like to order.

Tony considered that this daydream retreat into his work was a defense against his anxieties about relating to his girlfriend. He determined to focus his attention on their dinner together. The fish market was one of Boston's finest seafood restaurants and Tony and Nancy both loved it. As he was looking over the menu on the blackboard on the wall, he saw the entire Mills family file in. He almost choked on his water. Because of confidentiality, he couldn't say anything to Nancy. Nancy looked lovely, she was wearing a black dress and her short red hair stood out in contrast. Maybe Amy wouldn't notice them. The waiter seated the family far back behind them.

He had just started in on the mussels when he looked up to find Amy leaning down over their table. Once again, her face was too close to his for comfort. She was peering into his eyes.

"Why, if it isn't Doctor Potter," she glared.

Tony replied, "Hi. Oh, Amy Mills, this is Nancy Rand."

"If it isn't the beautiful blond Mrs. Potter," Amy said sarcastically. She then abruptly turned and glared at Nancy. "Frankly, I don't think you can sail worth a damn and I know you can't act."

Nancy was so dumbfounded that she couldn't reply. Neither could Tony.

"Ta, ta, Potters," Amy strode confidently back to her family's table. Inwardly, Tony heaved a big sigh of relief.

"Tony, who was that? Why did she say I was blond and Mrs. Potter and what did she mean by sailing? I never sail." Nancy was totally disconcerted.

Tony covered. "She's someone I know from Mount Sinai and quite honestly, it was as curious for me as it was for you."

Later he thought to himself that this was one that wasn't on the menu. Endive, yes; envy, no.   ✦

THE HISTORY OF THE PRIMARY PROCESS

In his "Project for a Scientific Psychology," Freud (1895/1958) discussed two kinds of mental thinking called the primary process and the secondary process. He listed the three mechanisms of the primary process: displacement, condensation, and symbolization. Before he settled on "symbolization" as the third process, he entertained a mechanism that he called "dramatization." Dramatization had to do with the mind's ability to generate scenes whereas symbolization had to do with the mind's substituting one thing for another. Later (1900), he introduced other aspects of unconscious thinking such as mutual contradiction, timelessness, representation by opposites, and concretization.

As these concepts developed, the primary process became associated with energy that was "unbound," the locale of the "unconscious," and the rule of the pleasure principle. Conversely, secondary process was associated with "bound" energy, the conscious, and the reality principle. Amy Mills's comments to Dr. Potter begin to make more sense in this light. In transforming Nancy Rand into a "blond" who "sails," we catch a glimpse at how "unbound psychic energy" flows. With respect to the unconscious, Amy is, no doubt, quite unaware of the origin of the content of this communication. Here is a closer look at the individual primary processes she employs.

Condensation is the process by which different pieces of mental content are brought together into one image or one sound. It is a composite picture. Thus, a neurotic female patient may dream of a tall girl with stringy, auburn hair and running sneakers. Insofar, as her mother is quite tall, her sister has auburn hair and her best girlfriend always wears running sneakers, this dream image represents a **condensation** of the important women figures in her life. Condensation is a mental montage. Psychotic speech often exhibits this phenomenon, and it is most commonly called a "neologism" or a "portmanteau" phenomenon. For example, if Andrew Stevens or Jack Barnes or another paranoid patient were taken to a VA (Veterans Administration) hospital involuntarily, and then asked if he knew where he was, a neologism type response would be: "I'm in a military industrial hospital." Here the Veterans Administration hospital piece of mental content is condensed with the patient's images of institutions that trick or manipulate others such as the "military industrial complex." The psychotic speech composite is his "military industrial hospital."

Displacement is a process, through which the meanings connected to one piece of mental content are disconnected from it and are reattached to a different piece of mental content. This is clearly illustrated by Amy Mills in calling Nancy Rand a blond. Mills disconnects the host of internal meanings she has to a "blond" or to "blonds" and reattaches them onto another piece of mental content—the visual perception she has of this woman who is with Dr. Potter. Behind what many would call "psychotic denial" or "very poor reality testing," we can see the displacement mechanism at work. Just a short time later, displacement gets called into action again as Rand gets accused of being a lousy sailor. Once again, Amy Mills disconnects her associations to someone she knows who sails and reattaches them onto Dr. Potter's companion.

Dramatization was Freud's first choice for the third and final primary process, rather than "symbolization." The difference is important, particularly in light of what the linguists were later to call "case frames." Freud (1902) noted:

> We must not suppose that dream symbolism is a creation of the dreamwork; it is in all probability a characteristic of the unconscious thinking which provides the dreamwork with the materials for condensation, displacement and dramatization. (p. 685)

Initially, dramatization was seen as the mechanism that transformed latent unconscious thoughts into sequential sensory images within the dreamwork. Symbolization, on the other hand, was viewed as a special kind of displacement that disguised aspects of repressed wishes as unusual pieces of mental content. With the possibility of developing a "universal codebook" for dream symbols and the excitement of unraveling the "method in the madness" of psychosis, attention within the field shifted to symbolization. Yet, was the method in Amy Mills's recasting of Nancy Rand as Potter's wife a function of "symbolization"? Perhaps, a better explanation is that her primary process of dramatization shaped her unbearable internal affect theme of "Envy" into a new script, a new scenario. In this way, the primary process of dramatization serves as the basis for transference phenomena. Rand becomes an inept Mrs. Potter as anger and envy work their way in the theater of the mind. In combination with the affects of envy, the primary processes of dramatization and displacement rewrite the evening menu for Tony Potter and Nancy Rand.

EVOLUTION OF THE PRIMARY PROCESS CONCEPT

By the time Freud wrote *The Interpretation of Dreams* (1900), symbolization took the spotlight in his general theory of dreaming, symptom formation, and the role of unconscious psychic determinism. Later, slips of the tongue and pen (Freud, 1901/1958b), and forgetting and transference (Freud, 1912/1958) were also understood in terms of their symbolic value.

In a diagram explaining the transformation of latent to manifest content in Freud's model, Ellenberger (1970, p. 491) includes dramatization along with symbolization, condensation, and displacement as four basic ingredients. He implies that Freud could have emphasized "thematization" as the third mechanism but found symbolization to be a quite satisfactory solution to the puzzle of the dreamwork. For example, under the influence of a feeling-toned complex, Amy Mills repeatedly dramatizes a mental scenario wherein a woman wants to "beat her out" because that woman is jealous of her. She imagines or fantasizes that Nancy Rand is such a woman and that Nancy is trying to undermine her special relationship with Dr. Potter.

The primary process concept then evolved into a classification system for thinking in general. Aspects of dreaming such as the absence of mutual contradiction, concretization of the abstract, timelessness, picturization, and representation by opposites were included in the workings of the primary process. With these conceptual tools, the expressions of psychotic patients were seen as being similar to dreams and were now better understood.

Merton Gill (1967) went back and took a fresh look at the other primary process mechanisms such as representation by opposites (a dwarf instead of a giant), the absence of mutual contradiction (it can be 10 A.M. and the moon is out), and concretization of the abstract (raining "cats and dogs" is depicted by canines and felines falling from the sky); he concluded that these operations are phenotypic expressions of the "genotypes of condensation and displacement."

> We have therefore uncovered no cogent arguments to extend the list of primary process mechanisms beyond condensation and displacement. I believe much more work needs to be done on symbolization, concreteness, plastic representation and hallucination as well as the relation of all these to condensation and displacement. For these two groupings may be on different levels of abstraction. In particular, I suggest that condensation and displacement are energic formulations while the others are, like the "techniques" discussed in the preceding section, what may be variously called formal, structural or phenomenological characterization. (p. 279)

Gill's use of the terms "genotype" and "phenotype" were probably influenced by the large role of molecular biology in the science of the 1950s and 1960s. His insightful analysis clarified the confusion surrounding the notion of the primary process, and his categorization into energic, formal, structural or phenomenological domains was conceptually useful. Though slightly different, the primary process of dramatization can be considered to be genotypic in nature and may be seen to have formal-energic properties.

NEUROTICS AND NORMALS USE PRIMARY PROCESS, TOO

Robert Holt (1962), a prominent psychoanalyst who was interested in language, extended Freud's notions of bound versus free cathexis. He noticed that the primary process does not neutralize sexual and aggressive energies, whereas the secondary process does.

Holt also used Piaget's developmental line for cognition as a model for his ideas and offered new contributions. First, he believed that the primary process and secondary process operate and develop in tandem rather than the one giving way to the other, as previously had been thought. This would have important implications for Potter's work with Amy Mills. The two of them would be communicating in both a primary and secondary process kind of way. In a similar fashion to Jung, Holt casts the primary process as a "kind of thinking," though, not necessarily "mythopoetic" in character. It was the synthetic function of primary process thinking that Holt believed was central:

Let us look more closely at the role of synthetic functioning in the primary process, returning to the example of magic. When we see it unmistakably in the play of children in the early verbal stages, magical ideation is characteristically "causal," implying a cognitive expectation that certain forms of behavior may be used as means to attain specific ends. But this is already a kind of synthetic function. It is a way of organizing experience into meaningful sequences, no matter that it does so fallaciously, or that its rules of inference are invalid—that is what makes it primitive and childish. Take away the synthetic aspect of a false integration and you have only disjointed fragments or aimlessly meandering woolly thought. . . . Assume with me therefore that the various forms of synthetic functioning are not an exclusive characteristic of secondary process but constitute something more elemental and inescapably human. (p. 374)

Holt is on the precipice of Freud's original dramatization idea here. He makes two important points. First, like Freud and the linguists, he believes that humans are "scenario generators." Thus, with the displacements and condensations of the primary process, Amy Mills also generates a scenario involving Dr. Potter and Nancy Rand. She synthetically links the characters together displacing and condensing important aspects of other pieces of her mental life onto and into them and comes up with a scene. Now, Holt would also assert that even normal individuals will process information through primary as well as secondary processes. This has significant implications for clinicians. Do clinicians process information coming from neurotic, borderline (character disordered) and psychotic patients differently? How does Dr. Potter process his experiences with Amy Mills? In the next chapter, we will address some of these questions.

Rycroft (1968), a creative analytic theorist, eloquently linked the concept of the primary process and psychic functioning to the general realm of communication. He refuted many of the original assumptions of the primary process such as these: The primary process is repressed or is lost, ontogenetically, to the secondary process; these processes are neurotic; and primary processes are primitive, maladaptive, and archaic. Rycroft (1975) was also helpful in recasting Freud's (1900/1958) earlier formulation of dramatization. Instead of the dream being a pictorialization of unconscious "sleep" thoughts, Rycroft proposed that the event-sequencing came first and that the thoughts came second.

It could be that the primary mode of mentation is representational and nondiscursive and we have to learn to spell out or explicate before we can convert nondiscursive imaginative activity into verbal discourse, in which case we don't do work translating thoughts into dream images, but the other way round. . . . (p. 16)

Thus, with Rand the blond sailor, Amy not only condenses and displaces internal, unconscious mental content, but she combines these elements into a scenario or a drama. Here is Freud's lost third primary function of dramatization. There are at least two actresses in this script, and one is striving not to be put down by the other either in acting or in sailing. One of the two actresses is married or attached to the actor. The theme is envy.

DRAMATIZATION: THE SUBSTRATE OF TRANSFERENCE AND REPETITION

Could this "scenario-generating" dramatization mechanism be responsible for yielding Jung's (1907/1976) "feeling-toned complexes"? Gill (1967) suggests that displacement of affect and theme plays a key role both in symptomatology and in the nature of repetition compulsion. Empirical and clinical evidence suggests that the dramatization process and its thematic mental structures are integrally involved with repetition and transference phenomena. In a myriad of fantastic ways, Amy's envy problem is displaced from new scenario to new scenario. A prominent Philadelphia psychotherapy researcher, Lester Luborsky (1992), has provided empirical evidence for the existence of transference in psychotherapy. He does this by relying on the tested and validated construct of the "core conflictual relationship theme." The elements of Luborsky's core conflictual relationship theme are identical to Burke's pentad, the linguists' case frame, and the kinds of thematic structures that the dramatization mechanism yields.

AFFECT AND THE PRIMARY PROCESS

As for the energic quality of the primary process, it is important to note that Freud (1895/1958) also saw affect as having a central configuring influence:

Pathways are followed which are ordinarily avoided; in particular, pathways leading to discharge, such as [actions] performed in the affective state. In conclusion, the affective process approximates the uninhibited primary process. (p. 357)

It may be that affect serves not only as a resultant of the primary process operations but as a force that guides their application (Garfield, 1986a, 1986b). Here again is Piaget's two-sided coin—affect and cognition mutually influencing one another. Emotion can cause the displacement of one set of meanings onto another piece of mental content; emotion can collect together various pieces of mental content into a collage and, finally, emotion can arrange the actors, props, settings, and actions into specific thematic mental scenarios. Professor Luc Ciompi (1994), a gifted clinician and scholar in Switzerland, has followed closely in the tradition of Bleuler and Jung in the development of his concept of "affect logic":

> . . . the focus of attention is continuously conditioned by emotional states. Therefore, these have a decisive influence on selection and linkage of relevant cognitive stimuli. . . . Secondly, storage and remobilization of cognitive material is state-dependent . . . cognitive information without a specific emotional connotation is hardly noticed nor stored and state-specific memories are remobilized in corresponding moods. (p. 9)

Thus, emotion configures memory and all cognitive phenomena—primary or secondary.

A well-known self psychology psychoanalyst, Joseph Lichtenberg (1992) reviewed the role of what he calls "model scenes" in psychoanalysis and the central role that affect plays in their construction. Model scenes are memory structures that impact significantly on behavior. He comes to an understanding of what motivates the patient through a window of key affect situations. Some of these experiences are preverbal and, thus, both the body and motor (procedural) memory come into play with respect to the psychological structure of these model scenes: "Longitudinally, affects provide the principal thread linking infants early presymbolic experiences, alone and with others, to later, more cognitively organized experiences" (p. 260).

With echoes of Jung (1907/1976), Lichtenberg notes that an "event achieves significance when it is amplified by an affective response. Psychological magnification occurs through the coassembly of similarly affect-laden experiences into model scenes" (p. 260).

Where does a primary process mode of thinking fit into this formulation? Lichtenberg covers Tomkins's (1962) theory of affect and is interested by Tomkins's rules for why certain positive scenes are linked to each other based on small variations in attributes and certain negative scenes are linked to each other based on analogy. Lichtenberg notes that the former is like secondary process and the latter is like primary processing. Thus, affect forms the glue of the psychic assembly and "primary process more fluidly displaces from one element to another, condenses the nonessentially related and gives double meanings in the form of symbols to the metaphorically relatable" (p. 264).

With her opening chief complaint, it is clear that Amy Mills is a metaphor crafter. Thus far, significant overlap can be seen between the linguists' notion of case frame, Kenneth Burke's grammar of motives, Piaget's schematization, the idea of the "thematic," and the primary process of dramatization. Metaphor making may be another form variety of this primary human mental function. And affect, in all of these, is seen as having a major impact on the shape this kind of primary processing takes. Siegelman (1990) following Jung, Freud, Rycroft, and the linguist, Lakoff, also points to the essential role that affect plays in metaphor making in psychoanalysis:

> My two decades of experience with patients have shown me that salient metaphors, or those that can be made salient through exploration, have three important characteristics:
>
> 1. They often . . . represent "the outcropping of an unconscious fantasy."
> 2. They combine the abstract and the concrete in a special way, enabling us to go from the known and the sensed to the unknown and the symbolic.
> 3. They achieve this combination in a way that typically arises from and produces strong feeling . . . (p. ix)

Feeling envied, is for Amy Mills, like "arsenic." Dr. Potter was first led into a web (a "feeling-toned complex") of connections to this particular deadly and poisonous affect in Amy's chief complaint. Remember back to the Shakespearean quote of envy being like arsenic and old lace. Along with poison, another new web is spun through Amy's reference to "old lace." *Arsenic and Old Lace* was the name of a 1940s Broadway show. Here is delicate cloth. Amy had aspired to be an actress. Potter's somewhat jolting, bouncing around is then tied together by Amy's using the metaphors one after the other and a larger web of a Broadway show raises the curtain on the chief complaint of this woman who has had her acting aspirations destroyed by an intolerable degree of envy. At the restaurant, Amy, again, throws out her fixed internal feelings and transfers them onto Nancy Rand.

Although dramatization casts an enchanting spell in the rendition of Amy Mills's psychosis, the clinician should be reminded of Carl Jung's famous advice to the author, James Joyce (Sass, 1992). Joyce had read Jung's written essays comparing his novels to the productions of psychosis; thus when Joyce's daughter Lucia became psychotic, he took her to see Jung. Jung evaluated the young woman and determined that she had dementia praecox. Much distraught, Joyce argued that perhaps, like himself, Lucia was a gifted, misunderstood artist. Although Jung did admit that there was a great bit of creativity to her neologisms, he emphasized that these were random rather than crafted words. Jung further offered the analogy that while the famous author and his daughter were both heading to the bottom of the same river, there was a crucial difference: The father was diving while the daughter was falling.

AFTER THE FALL: USING PRIMARY PROCESS TOOLS

After grasping the feeling-toned theme and seeing it operate in detail in the precipitating event, the clinician must look carefully as it replays itself over and over again in the productions of psychosis. For example, a therapist sees a charismatic 24-year-old man, Ed, who is in a constant panic that he is being watched and that his life is in danger. This is a fellow who always has done the right thing. He went to college because he was supposed to; he extended himself to others because a young man is supposed to be of service; he married a nice Catholic girl because he is Catholic and that's what he was supposed to do. Upon meeting the therapist, Ed says: "My folks want me to see you; I'm too paranoid and I don't know what I should be doing." He turns himself over to the clinician effortlessly, he is well rehearsed at giving away his life and independence. He is anxious and fearful. The feeling tone of fear is palpable. He describes himself as being a "heel."

He states that he had an affair and had abruptly left his wife of two years. This was the precipitant to this first break. He knows it was wrong. He is "so depressed." He worked at an ad agency; a 26-year-old woman, Maria, had been his best friend at work. Maria was a terrific listener. In investigating the precipitating event, the therapist finds that Ed had felt a "coldness" in his marriage, even though his wife, Sally, was everything he could have wanted—outgoing, a great homemaker, smart. She frequently would shop for small items with either her mother or his mother. Ed's family loved her. His friend from work, Maria, was from Puerto Rico; this was not what his Irish Catholic family had in mind for him. Yet, there was something about Maria—he felt so safe when he was with her. She seemed to understand him and believe in him.

Ed desperately wants the therapist to know how awful his panic and fear is; he recounts a situation where he and Maria are in a bar. They are meeting a group of friends from the ad agency after work. Maria gets up to chat with another woman from work and Ed starts to get nervous. When she is away for more than 5 minutes, he feels that everyone in the bar is staring at him and he worries that they are plotting against him. He insists that they leave and Maria is befuddled. His sense of being watched and his fear of being plotted against waxes and wanes. Even when Maria is constantly by his side, he can experience this fear. When they enter a new neighborhood with which Ed is unfamiliar, Ed says that he gets petrified. By empathically placing himself in Ed's position, the therapist begins to unearth the affective elements. Ed fears newness and yet, he can't tolerate blind obedience to something or someone he doesn't believe in. Furthermore, he doesn't believe in himself.

What strikes the clinician as interesting is that Ed's parents had hooked him up with two psychiatrists before but Ed never followed through with them. The therapist can sense the primary process at work. Unbearable affect is displaced from one group onto another. Was this his way of declaring independence? The new clinician might conclude that it is important to be available but not at the expense of Ed's own independent decision making. To leave him alone, as Maria has at times, doesn't work. To take over for him as his folks and Sally had, doesn't work. Scenarios of dependence and independence are generated. The primary process of dramatization brings them into bold relief. How to be with him and at the same time let him alone?

Ed's relationship with Maria is an interesting mix as well. Several key features are conjoined in his choice of her as new girlfriend under the process of condensation. Maria is different; she is from a different culture. Maria is the same; she is Catholic. He can feel very safe with her, but at times, even her presence does not guarantee a feeling of safety. In this way, the feeling-toned complex of fear over abandonment and anger over subjugation condense together in Maria. Later, the therapist finds that Ed has had a rather unique relationship with his dad. On the one hand, his dad was an admirable man, a true intellectual and scholar. Ed's dad told him that he wanted the best for Ed; yet, Ed informs you that his father never seemed to want to be around Ed. To go to a museum, yes; to play ball or to see the artwork that Ed had created, no.

With this history as confirmation of the unbearable affect of disappointment, the therapist realizes that the theme may easily get redramatized in the transference. What price will the clinician's friendship be? With the primary processes in the therapist's armamentarium, he is forewarned of pitfalls that may lay ahead.

Iris is our next patient. She is infamous throughout the hospital for acting-out. Clinicians know that she upsets people because she has been labeled as a "bad borderline." When the therapist meets Iris, she tries to kiss him and she tells him that she has heard that he is the best doctor in the hospital. Her affective instability is poorly controlled with adequate doses of lithium and carbamazepine. Others frequently have put her on neuroleptics and she shows signs of mild tardive dyskinesia. Iris states that she got readmitted this time because she got into a fight with her mother. Her mother owns a three-flat apartment building; her mom lives on the third floor and Iris lives on the second floor. She knows the clinician can help her get out of the hospital. She wants a boyfriend. She wants a baby. She had a baby when she was 17, but her mother made her give it away. That was the time of her first hospitalization. Now she's 40 years old.

The therapist inquires about the content of her fight with her mother. She says that the woman is too pushy and has a big mouth. Iris can't recall the details; it had something to do with cleaning up or paying some small bill. Iris threw a chair through the window, and her mom called the police. Iris says she shouldn't have done it, but her mom made her angry. The therapist is, rightfully, reticent to tell Iris what to do.

Let's say that the interview is on the inpatient unit and that when Iris is asked about the baby, she gets upset, then sad, and then begins to say "Humpty-Dumpty sat on a chair; Humpty-Dumpty had ugly hair (she pulls at her hair); Humpty-Dumpty had a big mouth of shit." The inquiry about the baby is a kind of continuous word association test (Jung, 1907/1976). Clearly, the baby topic wasn't sitting well. The loss and sadness are unbearable and rage is the result.

Iris's response is better understood under the microscope of the primary process. It was a condensation of many ingredients: a children's rhyme—with her as the baby (pulling on her hair) and in reference to her baby that she was forced to give away. Also, in the mix was a sense of herself of being ugly (this was new information). She identified herself with Humpty-Dumpty, which might mean that she experienced herself as having been and perhaps, as being, fragile/breakable. The reference to the big mouth may have referred to her experience with her mom and, potentially, an identification with her mom. Again, the feeling tone was one of sadness followed by rage.

Finally, the condensation may also have served as a warning to the therapist to not be too hopeful since the unspoken aspect of the rhyme was that all the king's men could not put Humpty back together again. Affect works its way through the primary process, first selecting items connected to sadness and then items connected to rage. As the chair through the window showed, Iris was quite capable of a very destructive rage. A primary process production allows the clinician, when viewing the rhyme as a condensation, to tease out elements that may prove extremely helpful. Forewarned is forearmed.

In summary, unbearable affect can be readily discerned in the clinician's reading of the patient's presentation. Various aspects of the chief complaint and the template of the precipitating event make it possible to empathically identify the central "core conflictual relationship theme" (Luborsky, 1992). Moving behind the initial presentation, clinicians have a better guide to psychotherapy with patients in psychosis when the mental machinery of the primary process is utilized to plot the current location and past travels of the patient. Knowing how memory, cognition, and perception can displace one from another or how they can condense together makes the forms and transformations of affect visible. Seeing symbolization and dramatization at work prepares clinicians for the transferences and countertransferences that are inevitable results of unbearable affect in the therapeutic milieu.

SECTION II
AFFECT THERAPEUTICS

5

COUNTERTRANSFERENCE: THE TRANSMISSION OF AFFECT

THE TRANSMISSION OF AFFECT: A PAINTING BY PICASSO

This couldn't be happening. This was the worst. The first time was nowhere near as bad as this time. Tony shifted uncomfortably in his seat and tried to think back to the first time, about a month ago. Then, like now, he was in session with Amy Mills. He couldn't quite remember what she was talking about then. It was right before he was going on vacation for two weeks and now he had been back for about one week. What he had noticed then shocked him.

Amy had been talking about one of her new girlfriends from the day program at the hospital, and Tony noticed that her face looked funny to him. It was not a weird smile or some inappropriate affect whereby her words were saying one thing and her facial expressions another. No, it had been quite different. It was as if her forehead was slightly off to one side, her eyes and nose off to the other side—kind of askew—and her mouth and chin were off to the first side again. Her face was out of joint. At that time, Tony had blinked a couple of times thinking that maybe he was weary, and in fact, Amy's face had returned to proper alignment. Yet, later in that same session, it had happened again. What was going on?

Could he have developed temporal lobe epilepsy? Certainly, these kinds of perceptual abnormalities are common in that kind of illness. Maybe he was getting multiple sclerosis. Yet, there was something disturbingly familiar about the way her face looked in those few abnormal snapshots of misperception. Later, he realized that he had seen this kind of misalignment before in a painting by Picasso. A painting by Picasso. Tony knew this meant something but he wasn't sure what.

Yet, today was far worse.

"I'm so glad you're back, Dr. Potter." Amy smiled.

"You missed me," Tony stated.

"Oh yes, I really missed you." There was a long pause and she looked at him sheepishly. "I particularly missed your penis. . . . How very much I missed it. Being able to suck on it."

Tony became very uncomfortable and wondered if this had to do with her being angry at him for his having gone on vacation.

"How did you feel without me?" he ventured.

"Very empty" she replied. "I wanted so much to suck on your penis and to rub your balls and to make you feel so good."

This was getting to be too much. But the worst part of it was that he experienced an erection. Could she see it? He thought he would die. What did it mean? Was he secretly a pervert? He didn't think so. Did he secretly want to have sex with her? After all, she was very beautiful. Yet, he wasn't unhappy with his relationship with Nancy. OK, here was this beautiful young woman who was telling him that she wanted so much to make him feel good sexually. Who wouldn't find that titillating? But actually, it made him feel embarrassed and very physically uncomfortable.

It wasn't so much that Tony was worried that he was going to cross some sexual boundary, even though he knew that many male psychiatrists had sexually exploited their patients. He knew he had good boundaries. It was more that someone was going to notice that this unbearable sexual material had stimulated him, against all his willpower, and that he would be found out and embarrassed, humiliated, perhaps, kicked out of the residency.

"Would you like me to suck on your penis?" Amy asked.

"What would that do for you?" Tony queried.

His erection had not gone away despite his willing it to do so.

"It would fill me up inside. I could have your baby in my stomach." She took on a reflective look.

"Would that make you feel less empty?" he asked.

"Yes," she replied and she sat back in her seat. She looked sad.

Tony noticed that his erection was going away and he decided that this was no time to let up on her. He feared that if he didn't pursue her feelings with her that he would be out of control for the entire session.

"What is that emptiness in your stomach like for you?" he questioned.

"It's like a big hole in me. Like when my mother wasn't there. Either she'd look down her long beautiful nose at me or she would hide. Hide from it all—not be there at all."

Amy looked off with a despondent look on her face. Tony knew that he had been saved here. His erection had subsided. Now he just felt exhausted.

It was as though his body had been temporarily taken over and used for someone else's purpose. He wondered if her father had abused her and if her mother had pulled an ostrichlike move—buried her head in the sand. Amy had talked before about her father and his erratic nature. Both she and her sister had been subjugated to his sadistic and erratic will. Mr. Mills would toss food out the dining room window if it did not please him. He gave the two girls laxatives on a daily basis and weighed them so they would be like "perfect pictures" in their appearances. Perfect pictures. His session from before his vacation came back to him. What would it take to please him? To please the big guy. Tony remembered that his own father would take him to art museums and have him study the Picassos. His dad would then quiz him. What did it take to please the big guy? The sentence went over and over in Tony's head. Tony suspected that his countertransference misperceptions and sensations were part of a transference-countertransference reverberation.

Tony decided to take a risk. If he asked her if her father had sexually abused her, she might say "no" in order to defend both her father, historically, and Tony, now, as the transference figure. So he took a slightly different tack.

"Was your father sexually interested in you?" he asked.

"I don't think he was . . ." she continued, ". . . well, there was one night, when he came home drunk, and he came up the stairs and he was cursing and, luckily, he passed by my sister's room . . . and he came into my room. I pretended to be sleeping. He still came in and he lay down on my bed next to me—stinking of alcohol. He rolled over on top of me and I think he had an erection. I was so disgusted that I pretended to wake up and I yelled 'Daddy!' and he rolled off of me and left the room."

Amy was back in the therapy now, remembering her past, thinking about it. Time was up. He had noted in his mind her comment that "luckily, he passed by" her sister's room. Had Amy concluded that her father had sexually abused her sister? Did her sister envy Amy her innocence? Had they ever talked about it? Tony decided that now was not the time to discuss this. He let the silence hang there for a little bit before he said, "We'll talk more later this week."   ✦

THE TRANSMISSION OF EMOTION: COUNTERTRANSFERENCE

Dr. Potter's unusual and disturbing experiences while treating Amy Mills fall under the general heading of the therapist's response to the patient. Insofar as these responses were outside Tony's control or initial awareness, they can be considered countertransference. But what do these kinds of responses mean and how can they be useful in psychotherapy? Potter's first unusual experience was a visual illusion. Here, the real stimulus of Amy's face served as a backdrop for a Picasso-esque visual misperception. Next, Potter experiences another perceptual/ somatic feeling—the disturbing erection. Dr. Potter's understanding of Amy's relationship with her father led him to realize that these experiences during the treatment might have something to do with the physical relationship between father and child. Yet, somehow, he also knew that it had to do with himself, the therapist, as well.

Mr. Mills had wanted his daughters to be like "perfect" pictures. Certainly, the chopped-up face that Dr. Potter had seen prior to his vacation was anything but that. Had she been worried about Potter's leaving for vacation? Offering herself up to him for psychotherapeutic artistry? An unsightly picture that "needed" his attention? Some emotion gets transferred from Mills to Potter and is then displayed or dramatized in this unusual perceptual way within the confines of his own mental apparatus.

What is central to Dr. Potter's experience is how Amy Mills's feelings get transmitted to her therapist. He ends up feeling the way she felt—embarrassed and physically, sexually, uncomfortable.

THE THERAPIST'S RESPONSE TO THE PATIENT

Harold Searles (1965), an eloquent Washington, DC, analyst of severely disturbed patients, has been one of the major proponents of the value of the therapist's response to the patient. In a refreshingly honest way, he details how exploration of his own associations and countertransference feelings aid him in understanding patients. In a paper concerning the mental states of perplexity, confusion, and suspicion, he comments on his own experience of scorn in dealing with the bafflement of one of his patients:

> Another aspect of the countertransference manifested itself in relation to the intense scorn which he so frequently expressed to me . . . in an effort to become clearer and more comfortable about the countertransference . . . I tried something new . . . I let myself free associate . . . this procedure brought to light much material on the significance of this patient in my feelings . . . my associations indicated to me that I had hitherto unrecognized intense scorn towards my father during those years and towards this patient currently. (p. 87)

Here, Searles uses free association to discover his own feelings and backtracks through the maze of his own mental apparatus to arrive at how this patient has come to elicit these specific feelings. He goes on to note how addressing the issue of scorn and being able to be more comfortable with it allowed for the patient's mental state of bafflement to remit. In addition, Searles presents numerous other examples of using his own feeling state to discern specific kinds of conflicts and dilemmas besetting both his patients and supervisees.

In working with psychotic patients, many psychoanalysts (Kernberg, 1976; Modell, 1976; Winnicott, 1947/1965) have written about the utility of countertransference feelings in diagnosis and treatment.

Brenner (1982) asserts that the correct conjecture about the patient is the goal and that the affective responses of the therapist may help in the formulation:

> Other analysts have called attention to the value of an analyst's paying attention to his own fantasies and affective state as clues in reaching a conjecture concerning the determinants of a patient's associations or behavior. If for example, instead of following what a patient is saying with his usual interest, an analyst finds himself bored, he should ask himself whether this is because the patient unconsciously wants to bore him . . . and the same may be true if one finds oneself irritated, provoked, sexually aroused, sleepy or the like. (p. 38)

What kind of conjecture can Dr. Potter make from his experiences? Was Amy Mills "inducing" an erection in him? Was she transferring embarrassing and uncomfortable sexual feelings to him? Analysts in the Kleinian school, particularly John Rosen (1968), have been strong advocates of using the therapist's response to the patient as a guide to therapy. The notion of projective identification comes into play here; intolerable or unsafe aspects of the patient's mental life are projected into the therapist and are thus disavowed—but they are kept as part of the patient's ongoing experience through identification. In this formulation, Amy puts her uncomfortable arousal "into" Potter. By bringing up the issue of sexual abuse directly with her, Tony "puts it back" inside the patient. In a therapeutic way, the entity of the alliance holds this oscillation, this difficult affect state.

THE TRANSMISSION OF UNBEARABLE AFFECT BY DRAMATIZATION

As unbearable affect is conveyed by the patient to the therapist, a whole host of responses are initiated. If the therapist is to "get the picture," how will that picture present itself? There are three main modes within which affect can be dramatized within the analyst once it is transmitted from the patient. These can be termed the perceptual mode, the contextual mode, and the representational mode. As patients attempt to communicate that which is troubling to them, specific feeling-toned themes are conveyed. As these themes are filtered through the therapist's mind, the primary process of dramatization acts on the themes to portray or dramatize them in one of the three modes. Thus, dramatization is not only the substrate of transference phenomena, but of countertransference phenomena as well. Perceptual forms appear most frequently during therapy with psychotic patients; contextual (action) forms, with borderline patients; and representational (daydream) forms, with neurotic patients. Thus, a developmental hierarchy exists in the structure of primary processing, and specific experiences are elicited in the therapist by developmentally different patients. Although this appears to be a neat format, a complete correspondence between developmental level in the patient and mode manifestation of affective theme in the therapist is by no means strict, and significant overlap occurs.

THE PERCEPTUAL MODE

Perceptual mode responses in the therapist are visual, auditory, tactile, gustatory, or olfactory experiences. These fall usually into the class of illusions rather than hallucinations: hearing one's name called over the loudspeaker in a hospital when it was not; feeling extreme muscle tension in a muscle group not under physical stress; or, perhaps, seeing a patient's body droop or hands enlarge. These perceptual distortions or illusions may represent, in part, an affective theme transmitted from the patient filtered through the therapist's psychic apparatus and dramatized in his or her perceptual illusion.

The therapist's physiological and psychological state is the filter through which the construction takes place. By articulating the perceived narrative, the therapist may select out the affective theme being communicated by the patient. We can hear Dr. Potter articulating this narrative when he tells himself that Amy's face looks "like a Picasso." In addition, working with psychotic patients, who often organize their own perceptual experiences according to the dictates of affect, may tend to pull more frequently for this kind of perceptual affect transmission in the therapist. Both of Dr. Potter's disturbing experiences with Amy Mills fall into this perceptual mode.

EMPATHY AND THE TRANSMISSION OF EMOTION

Leston Havens (1979), a Harvard psychoanalyst who has written extensively about working with very ill psychiatric patients, has observed this kind of perceptual empathy in his work with severely psychotic patients. He gives the quite relevant example of feeling a burning in his own skin during an interview with a young paranoid patient:

> Recently, I interviewed a young man complaining of intense burning feelings over much of his skin. He had more or less described that an unnamed enemy had implanted radioactive material in his brain, and that this caused the burning. . . . I attempted to attune myself closely to what he may have felt. . . . and in reaction to his account of the mother's rejection, I experienced an intense burning feeling in my own skin that felt to me principally like rage; compare the expression "that burns me up." (p. 40)

Here, Havens receives the feeling-toned theme from his psychotic young patient and transforms the received cues into a perceptual mode. By selecting out the theme of the perception, by reflecting on the narration or dramatization of the perceptual experience, he becomes aware of the patient's dilemma as it is communicatively transmitted to him.

Harold Searles (1965) has also written an illustrative account of how, in psychosis, perception is organized by affective theme. He describes a young woman in a confessional as she sees the priest's ears elongate; the priest begins to look like a mule or "ass." In the analysis of her experience, it became clear that instead of her perception of the priest's style giving rise to a feeling state, the feeling state gave rise to the perception.

THE CONTEXTUAL MODE—THE BODY IN MOTION

The transmission of affect (via dramatization) in the contextual mode consists of the therapist being put in a specific situational bind by the patient. This occurs most frequently in treating borderline patients, although it does occur in psychotic patients. In the contextual mode, the patient's affect is communicated to the therapist in such a way as to generate the same unbearable affect for the therapist that the patient experiences. Two points are of note here. First, the patient is not able to express his or her emotional state in words. A condition of "alexithymia" (Nemiah, 1974) exists. Unlike Joyce McDougall's (1989) psychosomatic solutions, the patient does not put the symptoms into his or her body; rather, the emotion gets put into coordinated motor forms—it gets put into action. Second, through turning "passive into active," the patient puts the therapist into a similar contextual dilemma and, in this way, communicates to the therapist what is being experienced. The feeling-toned complex is evoked within the therapist because of the context generated by the patient's behaviors.

Otto Kernberg (1976), a well-known analyst and researcher of borderline personality disturbed patients, has noted that these patients tend to induce strong and often primitive emotional responses in the therapist. The contextual mode of affect transmission may be what he calls the therapist's countertransference:

> How are we to understand that the borderline patient is able to induce such a complex reaction in the therapist? The therapist's effort to empathize with the patient leads him, in the case of borderline patients, to draw upon whatever capacity for awareness he had for primitive emotional reactions in himself. This temporary "dipping into" his own depth is reinforced by the patient's nonverbal behavior—particularly by those aspects of it that, in more or less subtle ways, imply an effort to exert control over the therapist, to impose on him the role assigned to the self or to an object-image within the patient's activated transference. We probably still do not know enough about how one person's behavior may induce emotional and behavioral reactions in another person. (p. 180)

Another Boston analyst, Arnold Modell (1980), has discussed the use of countertransference in understanding borderline and narcissistic patients. In particular, he has described a variety of ways in which patients do not actively express their affects but, rather, transmit them through actions, unconsciously intended to elicit these same emotions within the therapist. In some instances, the therapist may be able to feel that which the patient cannot feel:

> This phenomenon is characteristic of certain borderline and psychotic patients where the observer may experience intense guilt, depression, anxiety, etc. which in a certain sense has been "placed" in the object by an unconscious process in the subject. This is the well known phenomenon which has been termed projective identification by Klein. (p. 265)

Here, Modell pinpoints how Amy Mills is able to put her uncomfortable sexual guilt into Dr. Potter.

ACTING-IN

In other instances, the therapist may not feel the intended affect and may experience intense frustration and be tempted to "act in" as well. By articulating the contextual bind that he or she has been put in, the therapist may be enabled to keep alive an understanding exchange with the patient. A good example of how contextual transmissions of affect occur follows:

A 43-year-old woman had been in and out of psychiatric hospitalization for 25 years. She had been diagnosed as having manic-depressive psychosis and a borderline personality disorder. She had been maintained on lithium and haloperidol for several years. She was charming, volatile, and incapable of being alone outside the hospital. Unfortunately, she was intolerant of others, so group living situations perennially failed. She had been in treatment for 2 years in the hospital when she got into a fight with another patient and was put into a seclusion room with the door open so that she might "settle down." When she started ridiculing the staff, the door was closed but not locked. The therapist met with her briefly at this time. She started crying and said that no one understood her and that she wanted him to understand her. When it came time for the meeting to end, she grabbed his wrists and insisted that he stay with her. When he said that he needed his wrists free, she said, "Too bad." The therapist pulled away and headed toward the door, but she threw herself against the door and would not allow him to pass. He asked her to move aside, and she said, "No." He said that if she didn't move aside, he'd yell for help. She said, "Go ahead." The therapist yelled as loudly as he could and expected the attendants to come bursting in. She looked at him and said, "They're not coming." The therapist said with a great deal of despondence, "I noticed." She looked at him again and he looked at her, and they both broke into laughter. He had been taught his lesson and was allowed to leave.

The dilemma of being held and yet not being heard was the scenario recreated by this particular patient's behaviors. This acting-out was not generalized but had as its intent a very specific ·purpose—to elicit within the therapist a feeling state generated by the context of the situation. It was the acknowledgment of being in the same bind that allowed the therapist to understand the patient's unbearable affect—a mixture of fury, fear, and despair. Acknowledgment of the context and the feeling state it contains is the key to progress with the patient who conveys emotion in this way. What is noteworthy here is that it is not a sensory or perceptual portrayal of theme but, rather, a contextual one that is transmitted by the patient.

THE REPRESENTATIONAL MODE

Daydreams are the prototypic example of the representational mode. In response to the patient's affective theme, the therapist forms a daydream. This kind of dramatization takes place within each therapist's specific mental makeup. The patient provides, through his or her transmitted affect, the skeleton, and based on the individual characteristics of the therapist, it is dressed accordingly. In paying attention to the daydream, just as in attending to perceptual illusion or behavioral context, the therapist seeks to articulate the experienced theme and in this way is enabled to understand the patient's current plight.

Beres and Arlow (1974) describe the emergence of an unconscious fantasy in the therapist in response to the report of a patient's dream:

> Without the benefit of associations to the dream and before the process of intuition could become operative, the therapist had grasped the meaning of the patient's dream and responded with his own version of the identical unconscious fantasy. There was a sudden awareness on the therapist's part that his inner experience, which seemed so personal and idiosyncratic, was in effect a commentary on the patient's material. The correct interpretation had come into the therapist's mind in the form of a fantasy. It then required a set of cognitive operations for him to be able to translate this fantasy into an interpretation. (pp. 38–39).

In discussing the analytic treatment of dreams, Greenson (1960) comments on the pictures generated in the therapist's mind by the patient's report:

> To work effectively with a patient's dream, the analyst must subordinate his own theoretical interest, his own personal curiosity, and attempt to make contact with that which is living, accessible and dominant in the patient's psychic life at the time. He must associate empathically with the patient's material, as if he had lived in the patient's life. Then he must

translate the pictures he gets from the patient's verbal rendering of the dream back into thoughts, ideas and words. (p. 412)

It is interesting that the representational mode of both Beres and Arlow and Greenson is visual in nature. Freud (1923/1981) and Fliess (1959) defined visual thinking and pictorialization as being modes of action of the primary process. Yet, it is the portraying or dramatizing of transmitted affect that is the essential ingredient—not specifically a visualizing. Illusion, action, and cognition can all dramatize. Kaplan (1984) has argued that, in both hallucination and imaging, the sensory substance of the experience is minimal and that its impact is effected by its being fused with an "action-meaning" trace.

In illustrating the uses of countertransference, Racker (1968) points to the value of the analyst attending to personal thoughts and fantasies about the patient. In describing an instance during an analytic hour where he worried that he had looked "bad" in front of his patient at a recent analytic meeting, Racker notes:

> She then produced many associations related to the transference which she had previously rejected for reasons corresponding to the countertransference rejection of these same ideas by the analyst. The example showed the importance of observation of countertransference as a technical tool. (p. 147)

Thus, the representational mode is a cognitive form that tells a story. When reflected upon, its theme may be instructive as to the patient's affective communications.

Since many therapists are aware that they may daydream in a session and that this may be relevant to the patient's presence, a brief illustration focusing on the transmission of theme and its portrayal in the daydream may suffice:

A 35-year-old man lived in a rooming house and had been dependent on, yet separated from, his family. He was what many would call a "manipulative help-rejecter" (Groves, 1978). He constantly felt that the therapist was doing too little for him and was certain the therapist would reject him. After seeing him for 6 months, the patient came in and was complaining about how no one understood him and how he was constantly misinterpreted by medical personnel and that the therapist had to explain to everyone in his life the "real story" of his situation. The therapist was distracted by his own thinking of going to his own boss and asking him for a raise. The therapist wondered, "What if I don't get it, how will I pay for my wife's college education?" In reflecting on the theme of the fantasy portrayed, the therapist surmised that this constituted a feeling state of bankruptcy and desperation. In lacking resources of one's own, one is dependent on the "big guy" to step in and save the day. This fantasy corresponded to the patient's affective state in the hour.

THE PERILS OF IGNORING TRANSMITTED AFFECT

Rycroft (1956) has noted the transmittable characteristic of affect. Tomkins (1982) and other students of emotion have also identified this quality. Furer (1967) has even likened it to contagion in its infectious behavior. Crowd hysteria or fear is an example; so is the emotion of surprise. Whether emotion is received correctly or idiosyncratically or is misconstrued is not the issue.

Primary processing is not abnormal but is an ongoing kind of processing that occurs in conjunction with secondary processing in normal psychic activity. In psychopathological states, particularly psychosis, it was assumed that secondary process gave way to primary process. However, with a model of integrated primary and secondary processing, psychopathology results from discoordination or disintegration in functioning. It's more useful to view mental functioning as having degrees of differentiation and integration; the shape and form given to experience will be guided by mental processes operating at specific levels of psychic organization.

As mentioned earlier, Racker (1968) coined the principle of complementarity in psychotherapy: "Every transference situation provokes a countertransference situation." Thus, what goes on in therapy belongs to the therapy. Clinicians (e.g., R. Garfield, personal communication, 1985; Modell, 1980) have explicitly or implicitly espoused this view. Langs (1976) has also stressed the importance of the "bipersonal" field. Dr. Doris Benaron, one of Elvin Semrad's most gifted students at the Massachusetts Mental Health Center during the 1970s and 1980s, made this a ready part of her clinical work and teaching. Thus, along with the patient's words and behaviors, the therapist's experience during therapy provides essential information about the patient.

Finally, a patient's functioning at a different developmental level—be it one governed by perception, action, or cognition—may pull for different kinds of responses from the therapist. Thus, illusion, enactment, and daydream in the therapist may become friendly allies for psychotherapeutic work rather than distractions or distortions that detract from the goals of the clinical encounter. Racker's (1968) comment is crucial in this regard:

> According to my experience, the danger of exaggerated faith in the messages of one's own unconscious is, even when they refer to very "personal" reactions, less than the danger of repressing them and denying them any objective value. (p. 171)

Is Dr. Potter laying his neurotic (or more severe) conflicts onto Amy Mills? Is preoccupation with the analyst being glorified in this exposition? Potter is careful to assess whether his thoughts are related to his own problems or may be related to cues from Amy. One cannot advocate that therapists burden patients with their own problems. Psychotic patients deal with enough as it is. But insofar as primary processing is a part of normal functioning, it can be put to good use. That we cloak transmitted affect with the articles of our own mental life does not preclude the drawing out of the theme of what is transmitted and portrayed. Amy's role, as a "perfect picture," goes a long way back in her history; it has had a profound impact on her and now has a profound impact on Dr. Potter. Unless the picture of her past can be understood, it will continue to haunt her into the future.

SEPARATING OUT THE THREADS OF COUNTERTRANSFERENCE

Sandy Fitzpatrick was recently referred to a new therapist. She had suffered a postpartum psychotic depression and had two unpleasant encounters with mania. The last one was particularly illustrative since it occurred after she had an affair. She tells her new clinician that she grew up in an extremely abusive household where her father used to hit her and her mother would discipline her by beating her with a belt across the shoulder blades. Her dad and mom were alcoholics. Although her parents seemed to settle down by the time she reached puberty, her brother became wild at that time and would routinely smash her makeup mirror and bedroom furniture. He would also try to beat her up but she could physically fight back to some extent.

Sandy had been a talented girl. She excelled in sports, school, and her hobbies. She was an ace pool player and a soccer star, and was an excellent ceramicist. She reports that her brother was losing to her in a billiards game in the basement of their family home and he went "nuts." He suddenly pushed her head into the wall and she was dazed, and he started pounding her skull, time after time, into the wall. She believes he would have killed her had it not been for her father who rushed downstairs and broke a pool cue over his head. After puberty, her father had stopped hitting her and her mother was mostly negligent. Another traumatic event she recalled was her brother going into her room and smashing all her pottery vases and bowls. She had made about 10 special pieces which she kept in her room. She was devastated and when she complained to her mother, her mother told her to get a lock on the room door.

Sandy met her husband, James, when she was 19 and she recalls that although she did not fall madly in love at that time, he was very sweet to her and he was huge. He had big muscles and she remembers feeling that he would protect her. She had "run around" with lots of different guys between the ages of 16 and 19 and had been sexually active. James had not had any real girlfriends before and Sandy was his first sexual relationship.

The therapist can tell that Sandy is unsure about seeing someone for anything other than pharmacotherapy, and she had not been particularly compliant with medication after the hospital. It is suggested to her that she would probably need to be on lithium prophylaxis, and she recalled that she had been put on it in the past and that she had stopped the medication, but she wasn't sure why. Sandy comments she enjoys talking to her new therapist about her troubled past.

Sandy confided that since her husband's travel business has become very successful over the past three years she has felt ignored by him. "He used to pursue me. Now I can't even get him to spend any time with me. He wants to have quicky sex, which isn't very good and I'm left at home in this large house, bored to death." Sandy recalled how prior to her most recent manic episode, she had gone to Florida for the travel business to learn about new airline pricing policies. While there, she was courted by a married man who told her that she was "beautiful, smart, and talented." She tells the therapist, "My husband never makes me feel this way—appreciated." She ended up having sex with this man, but she notes that it was mainly because of the attention that he paid to her. Back at home, she told all to her husband James and she expected him to be enraged. In fact, "He handled it so well . . ." After a period of time, she became progressively more hyperactive and felt that she was special and had special powers. She believed that the CIA was watching her and had a plot to kill her because of her special powers. She was admitted to the hospital with a diagnosis of mania and was treated for a month with haloperidol before she went off of it on her own because she was feeling "flat." She had not been manic or depressed since.

Sandy mentioned that since the clinician was a man who listened to her, she experienced him as a father figure. She had been upset and felt like she was wasting her time and money when she was talking about her past. But when she was discussing the problems and feelings she had about James, she felt like the therapy was on the right track. At that moment, the therapist noticed an odd visual illusion. He was tired, it was the late afternoon. What he saw was Sandy with her back turned toward him instead of her front facing him. He noticed that her eyes were looking out at him from the back of her head and hair—there was no face, nose, or mouth—just her hair and her eyes. After forcing himself to "wake up" and after blinking his eyes several times, the illusion was gone.

The next step is for the therapist to articulate what he saw. "Sandy turned her back on me, yet, she was keeping her eyes on me from the back of her head." As with James, she had appreciated the attention from the new male therapist. When she felt the clinician was "off track with respect to her needs," she got him back on track to focus on the difficulties with her marriage. Here she was "turning away from him, yet keeping her eyes on him." This was a betrayal with a twist, she was watching to see how the man responded. She turns away and acts out and still tracks the man she's hoping will attend to her. The therapist now realizes that the same thing was true between her and her husband. Her affair was something of an effort to get her husband's attention. She closely watched his response and was disappointed that he had not been more upset. This dramatization of the felt betrayal and neglect were also resonant with what had been learned about her relationship with her mother. Her mom does nothing to prevent bad things from besetting her—in effect, her mother turns her back on Sandy. Yet, mom keeps some kind of an eye on her, suggesting that Sandy get a lock for the door to keep her brother out in the future.

The therapist now knows that unbearable neglect and sadness surround this recent manic episode. How Sandy gets her husband James to attend to her will be important. The process of bearing intolerable emotion has begun as the patient has effectively transferred emotion in dramatized form to the clinician. Now these troubling feeling-toned complexes are held between two individuals, the patient and the therapist.

In summary, affect therapeutics begins with the sharing of affect and, in this way, countertransference can be seen as the beginning of the healing process. Countertransference has long been held to be an essential road map (Searles, 1965; Winnicott, 1965) to clinicians working with patients in psychosis, but here it can be seen as more. It is a sign that unbearable affect is now held in a therapeutic relationship. The therapist is drawn into the work in a pivotal fashion. It is the first step in a process where disturbing feelings can be metabolized.

Perceptual forms of countertransference may exist more in clinicians who work with psychotic patients. Paying attention to the clinician's experiences during treatment is a crucial first step. These experiences, whether they be illusion, action, or fantasy must be considered part of the therapy; they belong to the therapy. Articulating the exact experience is the second step. Next, the clinician can share the theme that is dramatized in his own experience with the patient. This does not have to be a self-disclosure. For example, in the case of Sandy, the therapist can say to Sandy, "Do you think you try to stir up the important people in your life to see if they are really paying attention? I wonder if you feel neglected." In this way, unbearable affect begins to move, to oscillate in the therapeutic relationship. As it gets discussed and "chewed over," it is less overwhelming to the patient.

6
THE FORMS AND TRANSFORMATIONS OF AFFECT

THE TRANSFORMATION OF AFFECT: JACK BARNES

Tony's preoccupation with the Mills case was temporarily diffused by his intensifying work with Jack Barnes. Here it was a completely different story. Unlike Amy, who could talk for hours, Tony could barely get Jack to say a word. As recommended by his supervisors, Tony set up specific times for psychotherapy with Jack, even when Jack was on the inpatient unit. These times were kept separate from the usual ward rounds, diagnostic testing times, or team treatment meetings. Occasionally, Jack would show up at Tony's office door on time, but as often as not, Jack could be found down the hall or he would show up 5 minutes late. Sometimes, Jack would unexpectedly appear at nontherapy times. While in line in the cafeteria, Tony would turn around to find that Jack was right behind him; sometimes, when leaving the hospital, Jack would be standing near the door to the parking lot.

In session, Tony would invariably have to ask a lot of questions. Was something coming of all this?

Jack: (mumbling to himself) What?

Potter: I didn't say anything. (guessing . . .) What did the voices just tell you?

73

Jack: Nothing (laughs to himself).

Potter: What's so funny?

Jack: (looking startled by the comment) I didn't say anything (stated in a defensive tone).

Potter: No . . . I just noticed that you laughed to yourself.

Jack: I did?

Potter: Yeah.

Jack: Maybe I just thought something was funny, I don't know, I don't remember.

(long silence)

Jack: Do you think you can feel alive but be dead?

Potter: How do you mean?

Jack: I don't know.

Potter: When was the first time you were dead but felt alive?

Jack: When I got shot in the arm, in the elbow.

Potter: How old were you? Where were you?

Jack: I was 13—on a class trip. We went to Washington, DC, to the tomb of the unknown soldier. I think one of the guard's rifles shot me in the arm—the elbow, and killed me.

Potter: Then what happened?

Jack: The bullet went up my arm and across my chest and down into my liver and gave me cirrhosis.

Potter: What does this cirrhosis keep you from feeling?

Jack: Suicidal.

Potter realized then that Jack's delusions and, possibly, the hallucinations as well, kept him from feeling suicidal. They were a way of "binding" the suicidal feelings. The feelings in his arm, chest, and liver, no doubt, had a certain sensory quality to them. Perhaps, these feelings in his body are sad or despairing feelings. Shot by a **guardian** at the tomb of the **unknown.** Whom can you trust?   ✦

UNBEARABLE AFFECT TURNED INWARD

Louis Sass's *Madness and Modernism* (1992) is a rich treatise on the phenomenology of schizophrenia. Early in the book, he details the elements of the "Trema" and "Stimmung" that herald the schizophrenic break. *Trema* was the name that the German psychiatrist, Claus Conrad, gave to the preliminary change in mood seen in schizophrenia; it is a reference to the stage fright an actor feels before the curtain goes up. The patient takes on a particular look, described as the "truth-taking stare." All normal emotionality is replaced by this particular kind of anxiety. The name of this mood is borrowed from Nietzsche and is the untranslatable German term, *Stimmung*. This is what happened to Jack Barnes on the junior high school class trip to the Arlington National Cemetery. The break from reality begins in a subtle form; we can see something in his eyes and his unique state is conveyed by his "truth-taking stare." Jack was overtaken by the Stimmung.

Sass contends that the Stimmung can be separated into four stages. First, there is the period of "unreality"—this is an experience where things just don't seem the same. It is like the *jamais vu* of temporal lobe fits (a person may have been in a place hundreds of times before, but now doesn't recognize it), or a form of the agnosias (inability to recognize faces or familiar objects) of the parietal lobe stroke victim. Things are not the same.

The second stage of the Trema is what Sass calls "mere being." Here, nothing has any more emotional value than anything else. Significance evaporates. An ice cream cone and a head-on collision command the same amount of attention. With this inaccessibility of emotion, Jack Barnes isn't sure how to react.

The third stage is called "fragmentation," and in this stage there is a loss of the ability to compare one thing with another. Parts and wholes are not seen as having relationship to one another; they carry a separate and equal weight. Hierarchy, in terms of time (one event in a sequence of events), size, rank, and inheritance (the cow being the mother of the calf), seems to dissolve. Dr. Potter's first encounter with psychosis (with Andrew Stevens) exemplifies fragmentation. This construct is also similar to the linguist's notions of object taxonomies and case frames. Object taxonomies are those mental cognitive structures that let us know how things are related to each other in terms of attributes such as size, color, class/subclass—our calf and cow example. Case frames are those structures that show us the elements of an event—actor, prop, setting, and so forth—Kenneth Burke's pentad. In Sass's third stage, these relationships break apart, fragmentation occurs, and thought/speech disorder may be the result.

Finally, in the fourth stage, "apophany" emerges. "Apophany," from the Greek, means "to become manifest." Now, **everything** is meaningful. No stone is left unturned in terms of potential significance. Each grain of sand makes a statement. For Jack Barnes, each of Dr. Potter's words may carry inordinate significance.

AFFECT AND THE "TREMA"

Sass comments that a transformation of affect is central in the initial onset of the schizophrenic Stimmung: "Normal emotions like joy and sadness will be absent . . ." (p. 44). In other words, emotion goes inward.

The German/European psychiatrists of the 1800s and early 1900s sighted even earlier signs of the fundamental role affect abnormality plays in the onset of psychosis. As mentioned earlier, Eugene Bleuler (1905/1950), in his classic monograph *Dementia Praecox or The Group of Schizophrenias,* provided clinicians with one of the first thorough accounts of affectivity in schizophrenia. He detailed the observable abnormalities of affect present in the dementia praecox syndrome. Bleuler included affect as one of the four "A's"—ambivalence, affect, associations, and autism—that serve as the hallmarks of schizophrenia.

Also, as discussed earlier, in "The Psychogenesis of Mental Disease," Jung (1907/1976) emphasized the key role of the feeling-toned complex to the mental life of the psychotic patient. Through the word-association test, Jung first developed the theory that in schizophrenia, attention is caught up in a series of "feeling"-organized ideas. Jung would give a stimulus word and see how long it took the patient to respond. He then would record the content of the response and look for thematically related responses. He would look for conventional or idiosyncratic responses. Certain affect-laden thematic "complexes" kept the patient's mental state either disorganized or organized along affective lines rather than logical ones. Jung postulated that the feeling-toned complex arose out of early conflictual scenes within the individual patient's past. With Jack Barnes, the complex acts like a magnet drawing mental productions down to it. Lack of response and decreased initiation is the result. With Amy Mills, it was the opposite effect—the complex spews mental content outward. Tempting as it may be to make reference to modern psychiatry's classification of positive and negative symptom schizophrenia (Andreasen & Olsen, 1982), an objective categorization of the symptomatology does not give us much power in understanding the dimensional influence of emotion on mental content.

Why is Barnes so quiet? Why is it so impossible to get schizophrenic patients to interact? This loss of emotional expressivity has been called "emotional blunting" by neuropsychiatric researchers (Taylor, 1993), and many now feel it to be the most reliable indicator of schizophrenia. Where has the emotion gone?

AFFECT WITHDRAWAL, AUTISM, AND THE HISTORY OF NARCISSISM

Psychosis was seen as a withdrawal of "narcissistic" libido from the surrounding world by Freud (1924/1961) in "The Loss of Reality in Psychosis and Neurosis." Narcissism, as a concept, evolved from the myth of Narcissus; a young man falls in love with his own image in a reflecting pool. The concept has evolved, psychiatrically, to encompass the notion of a self-love kind of energy. This self-love then develops into more mature forms, namely, a love for others. Freud felt that, in psychosis, narcissistic self-love energy was withdrawn from others and taken back onto the self; it "hypercathects" or overloads the ego. The patient becomes unable to relate to others as he is completely preoccupied with himself; this reversal of psychic energy back onto himself makes him, in his own view, all powerful. Thus, in schizophrenia, the withdrawal from the outside world resulted in what is clinically manifest as autistic behavior as well as delusions of megalomania.

Sass discusses this "inwardness" that is typical of schizophrenia and illustrates how emotionalism goes underground. Jonathan Lang (a patient's pseudonym) (Sass, 1992) commented in the journal, Psychiatry in 1939, "[I] trained myself to favor ideation over emotion. . . . to block the affective response from showing any outward sign" (p. 94).

Many other prominent psychodynamic psychiatrists (Fromm-Reichman, 1959; Klein, 1930; Rosen, 1968; Rosenfeld, 1965; Searles, 1965; Sullivan, 1956; Winnicott, 1965) have approached the psychology of psychosis from interpersonal or object-relations perspectives. Terms like "selective inattention" and "parataxic distortion" or complex, internal pathogenic objects and notions of projective identification account for the psychopathophysiology of psychosis according to these authors. The great interpersonal psychiatrist, Harry Stack Sullivan (1956) used the term, "selective inattention," to describe a state where certain events, people, or objects are selectively ignored, and emotionally unimportant things receive too much attention. "Parataxic distortion" refers to an idiosyncratic, unique, individual way of interpreting events or objects.

The pathogenic object theorists conjure up vast internal, unconscious scenarios wherein significant others or aspects of these important people collide and conflict with each other in a silent internal theater. Object relations theorists, who put forward the mechanism of "projective identification," have pointed out how these internalized, cruel actors are cast outward onto unsuspecting people in the here and now; this incites the patient and, at the same time, holds the individual captive.

Thus, an undesirable aspect of the self is put onto someone else, and then that person becomes a necessary presence for the patient. None of these major theoreticians and clinicians have addressed the role of affect as a central focus in the treatment of psychotic patients.

THE WORK OF ELVIN SEMRAD

It wasn't until Semrad's work in the 1960s and 1970s that psychoanalysis moved affect back into a central position in the understanding and treatment of the psychoses. Khantzian, Dalsimer, and Semrad (1969) distilled out three cardinal phases of working with psychotic patients that they call "acknowledging," "bearing," and "putting in perspective" the intolerable affects that have driven the patient into psychosis. Already with Jack Barnes, Potter has begun the process of "acknowledging" intolerable affect. Witness the transformation of delusion into bodily sensation and body reference. Notice how this is eventually transformed into a verbal (secondary process) expression of affect—a "suicidal" feeling. Barnes acknowledges his suicidal feelings. Where does this desperation come from? How deep does it go? Through what roads does it travel? Emotion may have moved inward in schizophrenia, but can we easily assume that it is gone?

FROM PERCEPTION TO SENSATION TO COGNITION: A ROYAL ROAD

Perhaps Semrad's most valuable contribution was his map of the royal road of affect in psychosis. The phrase the "royal road" has its origins in Freud's (1900/1958) "Interpretation of Dreams." Freud suggested that primary process dream imagery was governed by specific rules. By analyzing the symbols, metaphors, or dramatizations of dreams, clinicians could gain insight into the patient's unconscious. Freud's royal road went from dream or symptom (such as a "Freudian slip") to a clue from the current day ("day residue") into the past (elements of repressed memories). Dream interpretation was aided by the tools of the primary process such as condensation, displacement, and dramatization (symbolization). Ellenberger (1970) points out that Freud's royal road to the unconscious for dreams and symptoms consisted of three elements. First, this road was a "hermeneutic" one (dreams could be translated; they tell a story). Second, dream interpretation was "investigative"; it uncovered early psychic trauma. Finally, this road was a "therapeutic" one; what was unconscious before was now made conscious. Thus, that "pathogenic secret" (Ellenberger, 1970) which caused all sorts of psychic turmoil, could now be uncovered and analyzed away.

TRACING THE FORMS AND TRANSFORMATIONS OF AFFECT

A slightly different royal road was postulated by Semrad and Van Buskirk (1969). This route traced the forms and transformations of affect in psychosis. Semrad's work focused on the fact that the same affect underwent certain specific kinds of changes in the movement from psychosis back to sanity. First, affect existed in the psychotic forms of delusion, hallucination, and disordered thought. Here, **perceptual** forms of affect hold sway. Be reminded that Jaspers (1963) argued that perception was intimately tied to delusion.

Second, this perceptual form of affect in psychotic phenomena could be moved into a somatic bodily form. This gateway from psychotic perceptual phenomena to bodily sensations has as its key, the concept of "feelings." It is precisely because affects and emotions **are** feelings, that Semrad's road could lead directly into the body. Feelings **must be able to be felt somewhere** in a person's body. Semrad used this gateway in the recovery process. He was known for taking the patient on an affect tour of the body. In this way, Dr. Potter would ask Jack Barnes where he feels this suicidal feeling in his body. Is it in his elbow, his arm, his chest, his right upper abdomen? What are those feelings like? Perhaps it is a tingling in the arm, a heaviness in the chest, and an aching pain in the belly. Interestingly, many historians and researchers view delusional phenomena through the lens of abnormal perception followed by cognitive explanation (Garety, 1991). What we learn from Semrad's royal road is that affect serves as the soil of psychic phenomena. Sensation and perception are laid down in a bed of affectivity. In psychotherapy, psychotic symptoms become bodily sensation as the road from perception back to sensation is traversed.

AFFECT IN THE BODY

Spitz (1957), Sharpe (1940), and Freedman and Grand (1976) have all stressed the ongoing and important connection of affect and its symbolic (representational) value to bodily sensation in psychoanalysis and communication in general. Krystal (1982) has pointed to the important evolution of affect from an early form as somatic states into verbal articulations. Arrests in this development may result in psychosomatic disorders. Professor Ciompi (1994), in Berne, also emphasizes the basic psychosomatic quality of affect:

> Affects such as joy, fear, aggressivity, sadness are understood, in affect logic, as global psycho-physiological states in which "affect" means not only the subjective domain of the psyche, but also the brain and the whole body. Thus the notion of affects is basically psychosomatic. (p. 4)

In her exploration of the body matrix of metaphor, Siegelman (1990) pays close attention to sensation and feeling in the body as the source of future cognitive understanding and knowledge:

> All our later feelings of bliss and dejection have their roots in the nursery and in the body. Body experiences are so peremptory that they carry with them their own seal of acceptance as "the real." And because these experiences are so primal and irrefutable, so **literally palpable** (boldface added), they become the sources of our most crucial metaphors. . . . What is real is what is felt with and through the body. Thus, it is no wonder that these experiences become the basic currency of metaphors of less tangible states of affect (pp. 26–27)

We can hear the stamp of "the real" in Jack Barnes's elbow-chest and liver feelings; that his body feeling evolves into a kind of despair comes as no surprise when viewed in light of Siegelman's words. Bodily sensations and experiences are first preverbal. Yet, like the chief complaint of each and every patient, bodily experience also has an affective signature. Some are common; some are idiosyncratic. Siegelman cites Lakoff in looking at a common affect—anger:

> Anger is frequently spoken of metaphorically as heat. There is good ground in both experience and physiology for this metaphor. When we get angry, our pulse rate increases, our blood pressure rises, and we feel flushed and hot. Heat in a container under pressure gives us a number of ways we have learned to speak of the experience of anger. Anger, like hot fluids in a container, pushes up. One's gorge "rises," one goes into a "towering" rage, anger "wells up." Anger, like hot fluid, produces steam (we talk of fuming or blowing off steam); we can add the metaphors of cookery that also reflect heat in a container: seething, stewing, or simmering with anger, one's blood boiling. Anger, like hot fluids, produces pressure on the container. One can no longer contain one's anger, one is ready to burst with it. If intense

enough, it threatens to destroy the container (we speak of blowing one's stack or hitting the ceiling). (p. 31)

This description of the bodily sensations of anger hearkens back to the case of Andrew Stevens. "If intense enough, it threatens to destroy the container . . ." Like the mirrored glass in the Stevens's foyer, anger shatters the psyche into thousands of pieces. Andrew is left helplessly trying to make sense of the scene of unbearable affect; Donald Jones leading him out by the elbow. His delusional perception of potential persecutors is the result.

THE THEATER OF THE BODY

Joyce McDougall, a well-known Parisian psychoanalyst, has worked extensively with psychosomatic patients. She has also tracked the transformation of affect into the body. In her book, *Theaters of the Body* (1989), she comments that the

. . . emotion aroused is not recognized in a symbolic way (that is, within the code of language which would have allowed the affect-laden representations to be named, thought about and dealt with by the mind), but instead is immediately transmitted by the mind to the body, in a primitive nonverbal way. . . . (p. 29)

With respect to psychosis, she goes on to point out that

. . . when affective links are stifled, this rift between psyche and soma may concomitantly favor a break in the links between primary and secondary processes. (p. 92)

She agrees in large part with the Semradian royal road when she traces affect either out of the body and back into the perceptual forms of psychosis or out of the body, forward, into more mature verbal/cognitive forms.

When there is a conspicuous lack of dreams and fantasies in circumstances that would normally produce such psychic activity, this is frequently replaced by somatic sensations and reactions. . . . Secondly, when affect-laden ideas return to consciousness, the defenses against them may achieve expression in the form of transitory "pseudo-perceptions" rather than emotions that can be named and contemplated. These dream equivalents, which often obey primary process thinking, may also be regarded as "affect equivalents." (p. 102)

Thus, by studying emotion in the bodies of her psychosomatic patients, McDougall discovered that disturbing affect can result in the delusions and hallucinations of psychosis, or in the fantasy life and dreams of neurotics.

AFFECT IN COGNITION

After "acknowledging" and "bearing," Semrad noted that "putting in perspective" was a final road to recovery from psychosis. Thus, unbearable affect had first to be named; it had to be defined and characterized. Next, it had to be borne—first in the body and then between the therapist and the patient. Finally, it had to be put in perspective. That is, the patient had to come to an understanding of how it came to be that these particular emotions were unacceptable. The past had to be explored for complete emotional mastery to take place. In this stage, fantasy, daydreams, and associations could dramatize the difficult affect state. No longer were somatic or psychotic forms necessary. Yes, conflicts and deficits might still remain, but repair of these injuries could take place in the usual fashion; through an understanding of and healing of the self. We have a glimpse of the cognitive form in Jack Barnes's statement about feeling suicidal. For Andrew Stevens, psychotherapy is required to move his suspiciousness and delusions more fully into his body where he harbors his irritation in his elbow and, eventually, into a full acceptance of the sources of his untenable pain.

MOBILIZING EMOTION: PSYCHOSIS, BODY, AND THOUGHT

When confronted with affect turned inward as in working with a "blunted schizophrenic" patient, what avenues are open to the clinician? Is it a question of simply finding the right key to unlock that which is hidden inside? No, usually a therapist has to try many different keys before finding one that may work at all. Affect cannot be owned and borne unless it is expressed and caught. Thus the clinician is on a constant lookout for signs of affective life. Gesture, utterances, body position, facial expressions, style, and color of dress—these are the elements.

When the therapist is called to see a 28-year-old woman who had a diagnosis of schizophrenia, he arrives to find that she is catatonic. She's not only not talking, she's not moving. The clinician decides to test for "mitgehen"—this is a physical examination test for catatonia—will she allow her limbs to be moved? Yes, she demonstrates this sign of catatonia. He then tests for "automatic obedience": This is another test for catatonia. Here, the patient is asked to stick out her tongue—in this case, she won't. If she did, the therapist would ask her to keep it out while gently sticking it with a pin. If she had automatic obedience, she would keep her tongue out despite the pinprick. She does demonstrate "waxy flexibility," a catatonia sign whereby she keeps her limbs in any posture in which they are set. The therapist tests for other signs of catatonia such as whether she will echo movements or sounds spontaneously. No echolalia and no echopraxia are evident in this young woman. In fact, the clinician notes that she is not attending to him at all. Recalling Luc Ciompi's (1994) comments that attention follows affective perception, the therapist, at this point, wonders what kind of feeling-toned complex has got hold of her.

After a few minutes of sitting there, mute alongside her, the clinician decides to try an empathic approach. He tells her how intensely conflicted she must feel; being torn between these two unbearable choices. He is attempting to see if she is "stuck": Is the "complex" one that has an inexorable fix on her? Although she doesn't answer, she does begin to move. She begins repetitive, "motor preservative" actions, she starts kneeling, then standing with her hands held together like she's praying. She begins to mutter something about the lord. Now, the therapist feels as if he has some elements to work with, although she refuses to or she can't speak or interact directly with him. When the therapist asks her what she wants, he again gets no answer. He asks her if she'd like a glass of water and he gets no answer. She seems "avolitional." No emotion shows; most would consider her catatonic and blunted. The clinician must shift gears again.

Remembering that emotion transforms itself from perception to the body and then to cognition, the therapist decides to motorically join her ("gestural empathy"). To some extent, he tries to establish a therapeutic bond through body motor action. Thus, he stands next to her and starts kneeling and standing, and he makes utterances such as "Forgive me Lord, for I have sinned." He notices that the patient begins to pick up the pace of her kneeling and standing, in terms of repetitions per minute. He decides to pick up his pace, standing and kneeling next to her. Similar to Jung's (1907/1976) word association test, the clinician concludes that first his body actions and next his words have hit on an unbearable affect theme inside her. At this point, he adds in a few extra phrases. He says (to no one in particular) "I didn't mean to do it. I know I'm guilty and I have sinned." In essence, he has increased the intensity of the feeling tone of guilt and remorse. He next turns to her and says— "Perhaps, I should die . . . Perhaps, I should die . . ." Finally, the patient stops kneeling and looks at him. Through one of the forms and transformations of emotion, a relationship is now, tentatively, established that effectively holds unbearable affect.

Now that the clinician has her attention, what does he do with it? To some unknown extent, he has seized the feeling tone of guilt and sin and has reproduced it outside of her. Thus, her attention has moved to the therapist. The therapist next decides that it is best to keep the attention from refixating. One of the goals here is the active circulation of affect. The therapist, being somewhat theatrical in nature, moves toward the window and says, "Perhaps, I should throw myself out the window; I don't deserve to live . . ." The patient quickly answers with "You can't—what about your children." He has struck on another piece of her puzzle, yet he doesn't know what it means. Recognizing that increasing the intensity of his own portrayal of her feeling tone helped a few minutes ago, the clinician increases the intensity of the communication now. In this role reversal, he states, "My children might be better off without me—I am a sinner—[and, in a louder voice he repeats]—I am a sinner." She then sits down on the side of the bed. The tact of motorically reproducing her intolerable feeling-tone and increasing its intensity appears to be working in establishing a nascent therapeutic relationship.

The clinician sits down also and tells her his name and tells her that he can't recall the children's names. She states that there are three children, Anthony, Angela, and Arturo. The three A's, you say. She says "yes, my three As."

Here, you have discovered what Carl Jung had been trying to convey to James Joyce: "She falls; you dive." Unlike the situation of a countertransference response to the patient, no particular feeling tone is communicated to the therapist in either his perceptions, the action demands of the patient, or the fantasies that are engendered in the therapist. Instead, by meeting the patient at the level of a specific form of emotion (body movement), he makes an educated guess as to what is happening within the patient and he uses that medium to help the patient begin to acknowledge and bear the unbearable affect. It was the catatonic praying movements that alerted the clinician to the intolerable set of feelings. The feelings were transformed from perception into the motor system of the patient's body. By sharing the feelings with the patient in this way, the therapist was able to decrease the burden.

In summary, knowing Semrad's (Semrad & Van Buskirk, 1969) forms and transformations of affect allows clinicians new avenues within which to establish a therapeutic alliance with psychotic patients. Hallucinations and delusions can be deciphered such that real communication can begin. Knowing that emotion is inextricably tied to feelings in the body allows for therapists not only to track but to join with the patient in bearing affect. As shown in the preceding example, that body can go into motion with emotion, which may be a crucial testing ground or meeting place for therapeutic activity. Finally, emotion lives in the fantasies, cognitions, and daydreams of psychotic patients as well.

To help steer a course out of psychosis, the clinician-navigator must be fully attuned to what drives patients in psychosis. What do they see and hear? What do they sense and feel? How do they move and what do they think? By knowing their copilots and how they experience and are motivated by the storms at hand, clinicians are able to take up a meaningful position alongside them.

7

SHAME, PRIDE, AND PARANOID PSYCHOSES

SHAMÉ AND PSYCHOSES: ROBERT MEYER

Tony's work with Robert Meyer began in a fairly unremarkable way. Yet, it was an experience that was to imprint itself indelibly on the young psychiatrist's mind. Meyer had been admitted to Mount Sinai with a delusional disorder of a persecutory type. After his introduction to the subject through Jack Barnes, Tony was ready and interested to go to work. Psychotherapy with Robert was easy. This was an articulate, intelligent, 29-year-old married man who had worked in his father's lighting business.

Childhood Pride and Unbridled Trust

Tony discovered that Robert had an invigorating and developmentally advanced childhood. He had been an active boy, played sports, had lots of friends, and reveled in his job as older brother to his two younger sisters. However, early in the therapy, Tony picked up that Robert's childhood had not been completely smooth. Robert had to defend his father from the jeering of neighborhood children. The Meyer family was the least affluent on the block and Robert would make up stories about how wealthy and powerful his dad was when other children would ask why their car was so old or why their house was so small. Robert simply told them that although his father was rich and well known, those things were not important in their family. Robert even remembered one or two fistfights around this issue. Through family meetings on the unit, Tony learned that, in fact, Mr. Meyer cared a great deal about material security. Sales became an avenue through which he could realize these wishes and Robert's dad became a premier salesman. After a few years, he began his own sales business and became progressively more prosperous.

In school, Robert was quite smart and, at sports, he was quite agile. At home, with dad away from home much of the time, he confided in his mother and helped raise the children. He noted how he learned most of his values and ideals from his mother and his "real world" sense from his father. During latency, he developed an avid interest in cars and dreamed of being a race car driver. Car magazines and models filled his bedroom. As adolescence approached, Robert remembered his dad's interest in teaching him about how the "real world" worked. It was a "jungle out there," according to Mr. Meyer, and a man must use all his skill and talent to avoid the traps of other men. It was "kill or be killed" in the business world.

Emerging Selfhood: Rends in the Fabric

During adolescence, Robert remembered long stretches of time when his father would tell him that he was "stupid," "not smart enough," "not clever enough," or "a lazy fool." He redoubled his efforts to win his father's pride. Every now and then, always in public, Mr. Meyer would laud his son extensively, telling whoever was around that his Robert was, clearly, one of the most brilliant and industrious young men a person could ever hope to meet. Tony found this mixture of frequent severe criticism and occasional praise intriguing and, potentially, destructive. It had, in fact, confused Robert, but when he brought it up to his mother, he was reassured—"That's typical, that's just how your father is with all the family."

For Robert, the choices open to him after high school graduation were uninspiring. Although he was a good student, his true love was racing. He spent his free time at a local racetrack, and he enjoyed learning from a car mechanic there about the intricacies of design, engine construction, and driving. However, his father's "put-down" of the merit of racing cars made college his primary, if unenthusiastic, option. He applied and was accepted to a quite good local university. Tony could almost feel a young man's proud chest being pushed in; when a person "caves in" does the "true self" go in hiding? Tony wondered.

Mr. Meyer had acquired several pieces of real estate property and bought and sold a few small businesses; success had finally arrived. Gradually, the family became quite wealthy. It was the business, Mr. Meyer asserted, and an attitude about business, that allowed for the family to thrive. A new house, rental properties, private schools, trust funds, and expensive cars were all taken on by the family. Robert moved out of the house and into one of the rental properties—his dad had made compelling arguments about rent and tax deductions, so a college dorm was not an option. Robert followed a course of general liberal arts study; he liked the great classics of literature and good grades were easy to come by, but inside himself he was unsettled, nothing seemed to infect him with a love of life. He had several subscriptions to car magazines and did do a little driving but it was not "appropriate" according to the family's status. In therapy with Tony, he remembered the major event of this time being meeting his future wife, Miriam.

A Trusting Seduction and Subjugation of the Self

Miriam was a shy and quiet girl. Significantly, she was not Catholic, a fact that the Meyer family had difficulty digesting. She was Lutheran, and the couple was eventually married by a local minister. The Meyer family priest refused to acknowledge the validity of this marriage. After Miriam moved into his apartment and their honeymoon was over, Robert decided to team up with a local auto-parts dealer to see if he could help turn this local money-losing business into a profitable one. He worked quite hard, and after a year, they began to do well. During this period, things between Robert and his wife were smooth; however, they had little contact with the rest of Robert's family.

After about 6 months of success in the auto-parts partnership, Robert's father approached him. Why didn't he leave this "nickel-and-dime" operation for something really big? He offered Robert a job in his multifaceted sales business with the promise that Robert would soon become president and run it on his own. Then dad could retire. The switchover was difficult for Robert. His father insisted that he work as a janitor, a "go-for"; initially, Robert was given no decision-making responsibility. He was to "prove" himself first. When he would protest, the father would tell him he was immature and stupid—if it looked as if Robert was going to quit and go back to the auto-parts business, Mr. Meyer would change tactics and, in select public settings, praise his son highly and speak loudly of his son's certain future success in the family business. Tony heard this shame/pride trap again and it made him very uneasy.

Tony was not surprised to hear that tension between Miriam and Robert increased at that time. Robert was receiving a lower salary but his father offset this, supposedly, by purchasing stock in Robert's name. Miriam tried to encourage him to stay away from the family, but he was torn. Robert would have intermittent and occasional explosive outbursts, usually in frustration; a window shade would not go on right and after several failed attempts, he threw it at the window, smashing the pane of glass. Alternately, he would blow up at Miriam only to later sulk about the apartment in shame and anger. The business was always on his mind. He became progressively more despondent; at times, he even failed to take interest in sports car events, his favorite pastime. Not surprisingly, the couple's sex life floundered and arguments became commonplace.

Heroes That Fail: The Last Straw

After a year and a half in his father's business, Robert fell on a new idea. He would develop and sell a new household lighting system. He had heard of the process through friends at a local engineering university; he presented the idea to his father who quickly appreciated the profit potential. Robert was instantly made "vice-president" of the family sales business and set to work on the product. If feasibility studies looked favorable, he would be made president and father would "retire" to be chairman of the board. With renewed energy, Robert set himself to the task; he held long meetings, proposed new partnerships, and began an intensive self-education plan with two prominent engineering professors.

Although less despondent in general, at home Robert was still quite tense. He slept little and brushed aside Miriam's attempts at intimacy. He fixed on his new endeavor with an intensity that frightened his wife at times. He was determined to show his father what he could do and that he would earn his place as president of the family business. The oscillation between his despondency and his zeal reminded Tony of Mr. Meyer's oscillation between either extreme criticism or extreme praise of Robert. There was a certain instability in this kind of oscillation that Tony worried about.

Indeed, Robert's father made him president of the business after thoroughly surveying the financial scope of the new lighting project. In his first act as president of the business, Robert announced that the business should commit 6 more months to the enterprise, and if at that time no real product appeared viable, he would close down the project and sell back the already purchased components to the wholesale distributor. He announced this plan to the employees of the sales force. At this juncture, Mr. Meyer privately informed his son that he would not tolerate a closing down of this project. It had been arranged that Robert was now legally responsible for the entire business, and Mr. Meyer told him that he would make sure that the wholesale distributor did not buy back the parts should Robert decide to pull out of the project. Robert became agitated and furious with his father and said that if it all came to financial ruin, "so be it." His father countered that should Robert fail, he would arrange to have the business building burned down; the insurance agency would go after Robert with the assumption that Robert was trying to get out of the financially failed venture by destroying the building and collecting the insurance. Now, Robert felt completely trapped. Robert told Tony that his father was an "asshole." Yet, with this complete rejection of his father, Robert was at a loss. A new kind of anxiety set in.

When All Is Lost: Unbearable Despair and Rage

At home Robert became progressively more agitated. It was wintertime, and he commented to Miriam that he thought he had overheard two employees laughing about "the April fool," meaning him. He had thought it might also have to do with April Fool's day or some day that was coming up—he wondered what it was about but he hadn't asked. He remembered back to his childhood when his father would tell him, "It's a jungle out there and you can't trust anyone. You have to learn to read between the lines." He began to feel that he wasn't reading between the lines. At work, he would notice people conferring with one another and was certain they were talking about him, about something he had done wrong. Why wouldn't they tell him straight out? A few people, he noticed, used their hands a lot when they were talking, and he wondered if they were gesturing signals or codes to one another. Robert's worry increased greatly, and he was constantly questioning Miriam about what this all meant.

From his work with Jack Barnes and his experience with Andrew Stevens, Tony knew that a breakdown in relations with idealized people could result in paranoia. With the loss of his father as an ideal figure, this type of love would fall back on the self and Robert would experience himself as being at the center of all eyes. The rage he experienced was now cast outward as workers in the business became probable enemies. It was impossible to know whom he could trust.

Anxiety became the focus of Robert's experience. He was convinced that employees knew something about an important event coming up in April about which his father must know but was not telling him. It became more difficult to concentrate on the lighting project and Robert felt himself to be losing his self-confidence. On several occasions, while worrying about certain numbers he thought had an important meaning, he found himself crying uncontrollably. He became extremely wary of his father and refused to talk to him unless his father would take responsibility for making him so worried in this way. Mr. Meyer told him to "act like a man," and when Robert confronted him in front of the entire family about threatening to burn down the business, his dad denied it. Robert was furious and almost hit the old man, but sped out of the house instead.

Coming to Clinical Attention

Miriam, who had been hearing of the numbers and gestures for weeks, insisted that Robert see a psychiatrist. Hospitalization was recommended and family therapy was tried, but Mr. Meyer refused to participate. Finally in a meeting between Robert, the first therapist, and Robert's dad, Mr. Meyer again denied he had put the son in any difficult position, and the therapist told Robert he would have to sever all ties with his father in order to survive. He was put on neuroleptic and antidepressant medication, which was of intermittent benefit. Robert stayed home deliberating whether he could, at this point, "start all over from scratch." He worried he would misread anyone with whom he would work, in terms of their gesturing to him. His confidence was gone. He talked to Miriam about life not being worth living. She was concerned about his despair and the potential for suicide and urged him to seek follow-up psychiatric help. He hated taking medication and did not want to return to a hospital. He had never thought of himself as anything other than a strong young man—there must be another way out. When Tony heard about this, the despair was palpable.

Again, determined, Robert sought out his father at work and insisted that his father confess to the threats and acknowledge the pain and suffering he had perpetrated. Again, his father told him that he was sorry Robert was feeling so badly, that he would do anything to help, but that he would not confess to something he had not done. At that point, Robert went home, loaded a 38-caliber revolver he kept in his drawer and told Miriam he was going to kill himself. Miriam yelled at him to stop and called the police, and what ensued was, in essence, a stalemate with Miriam, police, and parents trying to talk him out of pulling the trigger to a loaded gun he had pointed at his own head. Later, in a session with Tony, Robert remembered that his thought had been "He's the asshole; why should I shoot myself?" Robert put the gun down and was taken to Mount Sinai.

Tony could see Robert's uncertainties intensify while in the hospital. Just by being rehospitalized, he felt humiliated and frequently conceded that he had lost all of his self-esteem. He knew that if he could only understand the meanings of the gestures people made, why they mentioned certain numbers, why he felt so slow, then he might have a chance of lessening his fear and anxiety. He was convinced he would never understand and he felt "like a babbling baby." Tony tried to let Robert know how much he (Tony) admired him, but Robert couldn't hear it. He was fixed on his father. It was a long hospitalization, lasting three months, wherein individual psychotherapy, more family meetings (some of which Robert refused to attend), neuroleptic and antidepressant medication were all utilized. At several points, Tony had the inclination to simply discharge Robert, to end the humiliation that being an inpatient was having on him. Similarly, Tony felt trapped by the hospital "powers that be" who felt that Robert needed to stay.

Robert's relationship with Miriam deteriorated—they argued incessantly as he insisted that she explain to him every last detail of every conversation she had—he was not sure that he could trust her. He wondered if she was conspiring with his parents and if she had stopped believing that his father was responsible for his plight. Finally, in a state of complete frustration, Miriam told him that if he didn't agree to stop questioning her, she wouldn't visit him in the hospital. That evening, Robert became exceedingly agitated, delusional, and belligerent, requiring that the unit staff physically restrain him and force medication.

Fatal Transformations of Emotion

The next morning, he informed the staff that his thinking was clear and it was safe for him to be unrestrained. He became a model patient. He went to groups, met with his family and took his medication. He told everyone that he realized he had been sick, needed treatment and medication, and he wanted only to return home and to work to regain his lost confidence. He talked openly with Tony about the difficulties that would lay ahead with his family and with his wife, and said he would just have to live with it all. Tony, along with the other staff, was mesmerized by this transformation. In their last session, Robert acknowledged that to a certain extent he would be a "second-class citizen." He'd been hospitalized and diminished but he knew he could live with this and adapt to it. Before the end of the session, he said:

Robert: Did I ever tell you about my racing friend, Michael?

Tony: No, I don't think you've mentioned him . . .

Robert: Well, Michael and I used to compete fiercely, but we cared for each other a great deal. He was my best friend. I can remember that on one spring day, we decided we would race each other on three different tracks. It was hilarious, getting all geared up, moving the cars, racing, and then getting to the next track. I don't even remember who won. Sometimes, we would be speeding alongside each other and there would be a moment or two where we could look over at each other and know that we were in exactly the same place, at exactly the same time. . . .

Tony: What ever happened to Michael?

Robert: Well, I stopped racing, went on to college, met Miriam. Later, I heard that Michael had died in a racing accident. God, how I missed him. I know that that's the way he would've wanted to go.

Robert changed the topic to his returning home to Miriam and his plan to return to the hospital after the weekend pass.

Evidently, the weekend went smoothly and on Sunday morning, Robert made love with his wife. When it came time to return to the hospital, he locked himself in the bedroom. Miriam, realizing he was delaying, ran up to the bedroom and argued with him to let her in, but he refused. When she ran to the phone to call the police, she heard a shot. With a different pistol, Robert had suicided by shooting himself in the heart.

Aftermath

Tony got the news of Robert's death that same day. It happened to be Tony's birthday. Tony's birthday; Robert's death day. It left an indelible image on the young psychiatrist's psyche. Tony felt that he should have seen it coming. If not from Robert's too quick "flight into health," then surely from the allusion to Robert's best friend, Michael, being lost and killed and Robert's comfort with this notion of death. Tony felt he should never have let Robert go home on a pass at that point. He should have protested to the end of time that a "second-class status" was unequivocally unacceptable. Yet, Tony's voice had been too quiet and Robert's had been stilled.

It was difficult to go to the funeral, but Tony felt he had to do it. It was a large Catholic service. When he heard "the father, the son and the holy ghost," Tony couldn't stop thinking about how the son had sacrificed his own life for the love of the father. Tony's anger came in the thought that Robert's psychiatric status had shamed the father, therefore he had to die. A few weeks later, the family gathered with a few of the staff from Mount Sinai to discuss their grief; Robert's mother had insisted. She forced the father to come. When Mr. Meyer's eyes met Tony's, Tony thought he saw the beginning of a visage that would lead to sadness and tears. But what happened was quite remarkable; Mr. Meyer quickly "shut it down," looked away, and transformed his face into a social mask.   ◆

SELF-ESTEEM: THE FATHER, THE SON, AND PARANOID PSYCHOSIS

Semrad (1969) cautioned that unbearable affect may leave the patient with only one of three alternatives: homicide, suicide, or psychosis. Some forms of affect are final. These are the motorsomatic types that result in suicide or murder. As Semrad and Van Buskirk (1969) noted:

> Once integration with reality crumbles and our patient enters a disorganized and exhausting state of psychophysiological pain which he never could bear, other solutions are demanded. All that is open to the vulnerable ego at this point is suicide, murder, or psychosis. Suicide or murder are the extreme expressions of affect (principally rage) translated into action; psychosis is the partially rationalized containment of the affect, the sacrifice of reality to preserve life. (p. 23)

Although Robert had once taken a swing at his father and when contemplating suicide the first time had thought, "Why should I die when he's the asshole?" his first solution was not homicide nor suicide but rather psychosis. How did Robert get to the point where his only options were psychosis or violence toward himself or others?

Garfield and Havens (1991) have pointed out that paranoid phenomena have, at their core, specific deficits in self-esteem. These patients are beset with two particular problems. First, they have trusted too much. In the past, the ownership of self has been subjugated to the plans of others; in the present, it often continues to be betrayed; and, in the future, it faces constant threat. Throughout Robert's history, one could see the implicit trust put into his father and the way that Robert's own self was subjugated to the plans of the old man. Second, in the midst of all this threat, these patients frequently have the experience that the "rug has been pulled out from under them"; Mr. Meyer's betrayal of Robert's actions as the new president of the company clearly initiated this fall into psychosis. With nothing to stand for and no one to fall back on, paranoid patients have lost their bearings and it becomes impossible to get back on track. Whom can you trust? Taking initiative, making choices, and the exercise of self-will are futile endeavors if the person has not a clue about which way to turn. Information and ideas about how to proceed are desperately needed, and yet "helpers" cannot be trusted. Garfield and Havens contended that paranoid patients have lost their internal guides; that is, values, aspirations, and ideals are no longer available to help set a reasonable course. Without plans of their own, these patients fear being overwhelmed by the plans of others. As rage is projected and despair advances, there is a silent, but potentially deadly, loss of hope.

TRANSFORMATIONS OF HOPE

Hope may be the most overlooked of affects. It is intimately tied to affection; hope makes affection possible. Hope, like other affects, has its forms and transformations. Perceptually, it can take shape as misidentifications. These are the visual agnosias to the behavioral neurologists. A doctor or a father is seen as a devil or a god. For Dr. Potter and Robert, a holy ghost is needed. Someone to feel positive about. Closely allied are the psychotic cognitive misinterpretations—the delusions. Here is Freud's earlier (Freud, 1900/1958) formula that dream and delusion both are forms of "wish fulfillment." Hope is lost, so some way must be found to fill in the gap. Somatically, in the body, hope takes shape as breath and air. Here the chest is the vehicle. "Holding your breath" is the expression. With and without hope, one is inflated (or buoyantly "elated") or deflated. Dr. Potter empathically feels the "young man's proud chest pushed in" when listening to Robert talk about his father's domination. Cognitively, hope has the form of fantasy. Semrad and Van Buskirk (1969) felt that both fantasy and delusion were the result of frustrations in affection. Perhaps, this can be translated to "dashed hopes."

ANOTHER DIMENSION: SHAME

It might be argued that the dimension of the psyche most responsible for paranoid phenomena is the emotion of shame. The "shame" theme was discussed in 1896 by Freud (1911/1956) who noted that paranoid delusions of being watched can be seen as originating from a lifelong experience of severe shame. This perspective was echoed many years later by Morrison (1985). Several other authors/researchers, including Colby (1981) and Wurmser (1981), have viewed the affect of shame as central to the paranoid process. Kenneth Colby started out as a psychoanalyst and then tried to operationalize psychoanalytic concepts. He was the grandfather of the science of artificial intelligence or the use of computer algorithms in modeling human psychological behavior. Colby used artificial intelligence techniques to demonstrate how paranoid strategies are called on in an effort to avoid shame states. A later psychoanalytic writer, Wurmser, saw "betrayed" ideals as leading to shame and then to paranoia. The case of Robert Meyer illustrates Wurmser's ideas.

"Shame vulnerability" is best seen as a **signal** of how wide and deep the problem runs. Attention to shame is important in gaining the patient's trust for developing an alliance with psychotic and paranoid patients. But shame, as an emotion per se, is **not** causal. It emerges out of the throes of an unanchored self. Note Dr. Potter's uneasiness with the way that Robert's father would alternately shame and praise his son. It signaled that the problem was deep.

HOPE: AN OVERLOOKED AFFECT

Shame, which has sometimes been accorded the status of the main emotion of paranoia, may in fact, be better thought of as a secondary consequence of failed aspiration or dashed hopes. This is similar to Semrad's notion, earlier, of frustrated affection and dashed hopes.

Can aspiration or hope, in its own right, be considered an emotion? Ortony, Clore, and Collins (1988) believe that it can. They proposed a theory of emotion that views affects as the results of attitudes, standards, and appraisals that bear on objects, agents, and events. In their theory, it is the consequences of events and the actions of agents that yield the emotions characteristic of paranoia. Hope (and fear) is viewed in terms of the anticipation of future events. Pride, shame, reproach, and admiration are viewed in terms of the praiseworthiness of actions of agents (self or others).

Most of the preceding discussion has focused on the actions of agents; the phenomenological observations of delusion and hallucination have lent evidence pointing to the "actions of agents" emotions. Somebody is trying to "get me." That somebody is blameworthy. Is not a key element in paranoia the delusion? And, more specifically, the delusion that other agents are responsible for things happening in the patient's current life? What may be even more demoralizing in the clinical picture of paranoia is the lack of direction that the patient experiences. The frequent misinterpretation of events or the fixed hypotheses from which the patient cannot seem to free himself, speaks to the loss of confidence in making real choices, to the lost self. Robert Meyer sees "no way out." Here we return to the existentialists. Without hope, one is lost. And without affection, one is hopeless. Courage and will dissolve; only fear and uncertainty remain.

SELFOBJECTS

Chicago's Heinz Kohut (1977) created a new kind of psychoanalysis focusing on the primary role of the self. He understood paranoid ways of viewing the world as emerging out of a fragmented self. Empathic failures and frustrations during childhood might leave significant rends or holes in the fabric of the self. Selfobjects, Kohut theorized, are unconsciously sought to fill these gaps. That is, important individuals and relationships are both idealized and taken in to smooth out what otherwise might be wild swings in self-esteem, self-image, and related affective states. The person's **mastery and control** over these selfobjects is essential if healthy self-esteem is to develop. As long as Robert could leave his father and go back to the auto-parts business, his self-esteem was safe. He could maintain some control over his "selfobject." Of course, Dr. Potter was a firsthand witness to the terrible swings in self-esteem and affect states that Robert went through in his dealings with his father.

Garfield and Havens (1991) pointed out that Kohut's selfobjects and ego-ideal understandings represent a change in theory, paralleling that which occurred between Freud and the next wave of psychoanalytic theorists, the object relations school of Melanie Klein. Freud's structural model of the three agencies was followed by Klein's (1932) notion of an inner world of object relationships. The agencies themselves were not abandoned but became "peopled" with self and object representations. In a similar way, Kohut's selfobjects can be seen to "people" the ego-ideal.

Also, the relationship between selfobjects and ego-ideal is one of mutual influence. As individuals move through life and adopt mentors, role models, and heroes, these choices are not random but rather, are consistent with the already established ego-ideal. Conversely, in the person's interaction with selfobjects, the ego-ideal becomes modified and shaped. New values are adopted and old aspirations are modified.

POTTER'S FAILURE

Dr. Potter wasn't able to find and secure Robert's dashed hopes. The patient flailed about like a fish out of water. Garfield and Havens (1993) have suggested that, in psychotherapy, the patient's true self must be ardently defended. This is accomplished by standing alongside him. The counterprojective statements of Havens (1986) are useful in that effort. Here, the therapist is no longer another "well wisher" whom one must also suspect, but rather is a staunch ally proclaiming, "The old man is not just an asshole; he is the devil incarnate." Rather than promoting delusion, such statements tend to minimize the need for projected rage. Havens calls this "empathy with rage."

Equally important, Garfield and Havens contend, is the need to lure narcissism back to the ego-ideal. Self-esteem must be preserved, aspiration rekindled, and initiative applauded. "Your auto-parts business was far better, far more ethical, more decent and, no doubt, ultimately, more profitable than your father's reckless company." These are Havens's "performatives"; statements that seek to identify and amplify healthy self-regard. Robert didn't need another friend to race cars with—he needed a defender who believed in him. With the loss of his key selfobjects, first his father and then his wife, he was defenseless and unable to view himself with any positive self-regard. Patients recovering from paranoid conditions go through three phases of recovery—recompensation from persecutory psychosis, reconstruction of the psychic agencies (ego-ideal), and then a development of the self (Havens & Garfield, 1993). Robert had not yet successfully negotiated the first phase.

A COMMON CAUSE: MANFRED CONRAD

Manfred Conrad had been seen for about a year at an inner city VA Hospital, by a therapist who moved to another city. He was referred to a new clinician in the same clinic to continue the treatment. In the first interview with the new therapist, Mr. Conrad noted that he had not developed much of a relationship with his previous therapist, a woman, over the past year. He believed that people at the Veterans Hospital had it in for him. He had been in the Air Force 35 years ago, and he had been married to a beautiful woman from Argentina. When he first met his ex-wife, he spoke very little Spanish; she seemed to be quite enamored of him, so he married her. Mr. Conrad is less interested in relating his life story than he is in getting the new clinician to see what a **headache** the VA hospital is for him. He notes that he went through some of this with the former therapist, "the little girl who left town."

The new therapist is also a woman and decides that an empathic approach won't work. Manfred Conrad will not want to hear that he must be disappointed in his inability to communicate effectively with women (first his wife and now his extherapist, implying that it might be difficult for him with the new woman therapist as well). Instead, the new clinician decides to take a counterprojective approach, moving away from Mr. Conrad and onto the VA hospital. She decides to join him in a common cause.

Th: That VA can be a real pain in the neck (getting close to the anatomy of his headache).

Conrad: You don't know the half of it . . . they owe me big time . . .

Th: Your marriage might still be intact if not for the stupid military . . . (reaching, putting the blame "out there").

Conrad: I don't know what happened . . . when I came home, she seemed different, I was hearing voices (looks at therapist, to see the reaction) . . .

Th: Could they have spiked something you drank?

Conrad: I wondered that myself . . . long pause . . . then Anita decided that she wanted to go back home to Argentina . . .

Th: (sarcastically) Great . . . nothing like standing behind your man . . .

Conrad: (somewhat defensively) She didn't know anything . . . she hardly spoke English . . . and I was in a panic . . .

Th: She didn't pull the "poor defenseless little woman" routine did she?

(Conrad is silent.)

Th: Women—you just can't trust them . . . they're almost as bad as the VA—sometimes worse.

Here the therapist joins him in his general sense of mistrust—the therapist can feel herself becoming enraged with Anita . . . the outside world becomes filled with people who cannot be trusted. This common antagonist allows the patient to become more at ease in talking; there is no pressure on him to justify his beliefs to the new clinician. The forces at work behind the beliefs are now free to express themselves. With this focus on the outside, the interpersonal field between therapist and patient clears; later, the locus of the enemy moves from the outside to the inside and self-criticism runs rampant in the paranoid patient in the phase of reconstruction. Depression will likely emerge.

CONRAD: PART II

Two years later, the new therapist is meeting regularly with Manfred Conrad. His fear of the VA has abated; no longer does he believe that they are plotting against him. He has revealed a great bit about his years since the service, his impressive knowledge of international politics; his uncanny knack for winning at the racetrack. While supporting himself on his VA pension, he has accumulated a sizable nest egg through his betting on the "ponies." This is a man who knows his stuff.

Slowly, over the past several months, he has begun to reveal his insecurities to the therapist. He feels he was inadequate as a husband; that he had a bright career ahead of him in the Air Force which he threw away due to his being "paranoid." He exhorts the clinician to explain his psychopathology to him. The therapist decides, wisely, to not take the bait and rather, to counterproject with respect to the past. Does Conrad really believe it was all his fault? The therapist emphasizes that powerful forces were at work that were well beyond the patient's control. Anita's relationship with her family was a silent but powerfully persuasive one. The Air Force had great difficulty in recognizing someone with significant intellectual gifts—the military has never been able to exploit great minds to the benefit of the country. The therapist has crossed the first watershed in working with patients beset with persecutory psychoses. Recompensation has taken place through the use of counterprojective statements. A persecutory transference has been avoided through empathizing with the patient's anger at those who stymie him. The therapist recognizes the emergence of the second stage, the period of reconstruction of the psychic agencies. Here, depression is prominent and the therapist wards off temptations to blame the victim. Self-esteem is successfully protected.

Previously paranoid patients in the midst of depression need ongoing support for a beleaguered self. The superego attacks characteristic of this stage can be fierce and the depression, as has been seen in the case of Robert Meyer, can be deadly. Clinicians have to be on the watch for suicide. How long does it take to emerge from this stage of reconstruction? Two signs are key. As Garfield and Havens (1993) have pointed out, a reembracing of old lost values and the development of some healthy assertiveness are indicators that the ego-ideal is back in action.

In this second stage, the new clinician notes that Mr. Conrad has started to reread Karl Marx and Adam Smith—he had always believed that a global system based on free enterprise coupled with social justice was possible. When he is humiliated by his aging mother whom he regularly visits, he begins to stand up to her and tell her that her rigidity, regardless of her age, is terribly undesirable. He also screws up his courage to tell the new therapist that he's tired of her being late to appointments. He wonders out loud if she has a problem with male patients. Persecutory antagonism has transformed itself into healthy assertiveness as the ego-ideal "re-minds" itself.

As will be seen in Dr. Potter's ongoing work with Amy Mills, the third phase of development of the self is one that applies not only to persecutory states but also to psychosis in general. For Manfred Conrad, his belief in himself will need to be solidified. The new therapist will be tested as will the patient's own self-resolve. The new relationships that the patient has made will become key in this regard. Given the changes, during this last stage, unbearable affects can more easily blend with other affects. Mixed feelings are likely. No one set of affects dominates the psychic stage. Manfred Conrad can trust himself to be more honest and he can once again trust women as they progressively earn his trust. The therapist should be on the lookout for new ventures or creative productions of the patient as well. These are signs of a new self.

In summary, the clinician-navigator who works with the persecutory psychoses has a tricky task. The focus must be not on the abilities of the single crew member on board, but rather on the violence of the natural world. To be allowed to help, the therapist must first stay out of the way. This situational alliance is crucial to the sharing of rage. And, as the patient begins to doubt himself as an able-bodied crew member, the clinician must not let him sink. Then the whole enterprise is lost. Rather, one must keep an eye on the hurricane forces that still lay potentially ahead or which have only recently been overcome. Patient and therapist are lucky to have survived. As a working crew now takes charge, new courses of action become possible. The crew can now, together, take a few risks as it becomes clear that **all** is not at risk.

8

EMOTION AND SELF-ESTEEM IN PSYCHOSIS

No Self-Esteem: Amy Mills

Amy seemed depressed. Somehow being in the hospital for two months had taken some of her dramatic style out of her. Tony could relate to that; his initial enthusiasm, the mission to cure, had certainly taken its lumps as well. His experience with Robert Meyer almost did him in. Where was that bubble of omnipotence that was supposed to protect us from the harsh realities of day-to-day life? It seemed nowhere to be found.

Amy was now "graduating" to outpatient status. Her rapid, pressured speech had been tempered by lithium. Her oratory and dramatic flair were now more subdued. Although Tony didn't believe in the syndrome of "postpsychotic depression," he knew that it could be the beginning of the down part of her bipolar affective disorder. Perhaps, she was just exhausted from the whole ordeal. Tony reassured himself that the lithium would help protect her from becoming neurovegetative. But it couldn't protect either of them from the distasteful choices of day-to-day living. He hoped that the old adage of "depression shared is depression halved" was true. Yet, would it be hers or his?

Luckily, their relationship was on solid footing and Tony knew that they could weather this period of time. Amy had decided to not go back to her sister's apartment. The interactions there were too assaultive to her self-esteem. What she gained in support, she lost in self-respect. Tony agreed with the decision. That left her with either getting a single occupancy room or with going into a halfway house until she felt comfortable moving into an

103

apartment with other young women her age. There was also the question of work.

During her twice weekly therapy sessions, Amy would intermittently come in and smile and tell Tony that he was her God. The smile was put on, it was kind of plastic.

Amy: Hi. You know how much I love you. Do you love me? Oh, I forgot, I should bow down. Should I bow down? You are my God.

Tony figured she was, in part, clowning around. Yet, he wondered what had stimulated this partial deification. Had he screwed up? Had she screwed up? Why at this moment did she need to revert to this posture of deference? Did it have to do with his one-week vacation? Was she afraid he would leave her for good if she didn't puff up his sense of self-importance?

Potter: How are you feeling? (He decided to focus on affect.)

Amy: Fine, my Lord. And you?

Potter: How do I look?

Amy: Maybe a little depressed? Are you a little depressed?

Potter: Depression is in the air?

Amy: (leaning back, kind of sad) Maybe so. I really do work hard.

Potter: There's never been a doubt in my mind about how hard working *and* dedicated you are.

Amy: Mrs. Leary doesn't seem to think that I work hard. (Amy looks more dejected—Mrs. Leary is the halfway house owner).

Potter: She really doesn't know you (pause). What happened?

Amy: (smiles a more genuine smile) You're sweet. I don't know. She asked me to do the dishes, which is my chore, which I did and then she commented that the front hallway was a mess—I mean, she made this "comment" to me, like it was my fault or that I was supposed to clean it up.

Potter: Whose job was it?

Amy: It was Sandy's job—which she didn't do—I mean I know Sandy has had a hard time lately (looks guilty).

Potter: Still—it wasn't your responsibility . . .

Amy: No, I mean, I cover for her all the time and she's so caught up with herself—I know she was sexually abused and all and Mrs. Leary can be very demanding. Sandy thinks I've got it made just because I got a job at Harry's.

Potter: Is Sandy jealous?

Amy: (with a quick glance) Maybe. But for Christ's sake, it's just a cashier's job. What I can't get is why can't Mrs. Leary see what's going on?

Potter: Maybe I don't see what's going on sometimes.

Amy: Why do you say that? You always see what's going on (smiles a kind of dutiful smile).

Tony realized that the God references to him were most likely in response to his not being attuned to what was really going on with Amy in her new environment and that her semidelusional references were attempts to restore him to a position that she needed him to be in, namely, "knowing" her. When he could arrive at a more empathic position, the "subdued" tone came back. He knew that for her eventual recovery, it was essential not only for him to label sadness but to be able to bear it with her as well.

It was not easy. Psychosis is more exciting and engaging than reality. It was one of the major pitfalls of doing this work—an escape from the mundane. He needed to be able for the two of them to find solace and asylum in the ordinary as well as the extraordinary.

Potter: Did I congratulate you on your new job? Harry's is a pretty busy place.

Amy: (pleased) Come on Dr. Potter, it's just a cashier's job. It's not like my heart is really into being a cashier for the rest of my life. (pause) Actually, I'd like to sing again. (long pause) Want to hear me sing?

Tony wasn't sure if he wanted to hear her sing. He was afraid for her—that it wouldn't sound good—that she'd feel bad, but before he finished his thought . . .

Amy: "To dream, the impossible dream . . . To fight the unbeatable foe. . . ." (Her voice was a little crackly but she started to really put herself into it.)

Tony sat back and listened. She was really quite inspiring. When she stopped, she wasn't even embarrassed. She just smiled. It was a genuine smile, one of satisfaction.

Potter: That was beautiful.
Amy: Thanks.

For the rest of the session there were no more references to Tony being God or "my Lord." Nor did Amy put on a fake plastic smile.   ✦

SELF-ESTEEM AND PSYCHOSIS

Amy's deification of Tony Potter was a small blip in the course of her treatment, yet it raises an important therapeutic issue. What role does the doctor play for the patient in the recovery from psychosis?

To a certain extent, Amy feels diminished by her new job. Yet, at the same time she knows she's out of the hospital and is moving on. She feels diminished by being blamed by Mrs. Leary and the old theme of envy and protection of a sister comes into play. In working with psychotic patients, one must never underestimate the importance of the doctor to the patient. Where is Dr. Potter in all this? Semrad (Semrad & Van Buskirk, 1969) commented: "The therapist's first concern must be to develop and maintain a relationship which will meet the patient's fundamental needs of sustenance, support and gratification, the disruption of which has led to a psychotic regression" (p. 31).

Yet, sustenance and support for what? Many analysts, (Federn, 1953; Freeman, 1963; Freud, 1896/1962) have pointed out that significant losses in self-esteem are at the heart of psychosis. Benedetti (1987), the famous Italian analyst who has worked in intensive psychotherapy with over 500 psychotic patients, noted: "There is, in the schizophrenic personality, a great loss of narcissism. . . . A main function of the therapist is, then, to restore this narcissistic gap" (p. 57). In Amy Mill's life, Tony Potter fills the narcissistic gap.

In his writings on ego libido, Freud (1896) identified the important role of self-esteem in psychosis. Self-love energy (libido) or what was called "primitive narcissism," cathected or attached to the ego and became "ego libido." As mentioned earlier, it was then transformed into object love (true love of an individual of the opposite sex) through the way station of homosexual love (love of someone similar to the individual). Thus, Freud envisioned the development of real love as a three-step process. First, "I love me." Then, "I love someone like me." Finally, "I can love someone opposite to me."

Along with self-love (which eventually became object love), Freud believed each individual also had object libido, which was mental energy that attached from the ego to outside people or objects. He postulated that certain frustrations could overwhelm the ego and cause a detachment of cathexis from the outside world, which would then return to hyperinvest the ego. The psychotic patient thus becomes consumed with himself. As discussed before, this was the formula for the autistic component of schizophrenia. As Freud pointed out, in this schema, no transference was possible since no psychic energy was available to cathect an analyst. Psychotic phenomena such as hallucinations and delusions were seen as attempts to restore some kind of relationship with the outside world.

Later, when he put forward the structural model of the mind (id, ego, and superego/ego-ideal), Freud (1924) considered psychosis to be the result of a conflict between the ego and reality such that the ego sided with the id against the frustrations of distasteful day-to-day life. Overwhelming impulses swamped the ego and drove a wedge between the ego and reality. Freud's early ideas set the stage for later conceptualizations of conflict versus deficit in the psychology of psychosis.

AFFECT AND NARCISSISM—FEDERN'S WORK

Paul Federn (Federn, 1953), a famous student of Freud, expanded on Freud's original ideas about the role of narcissism in psychosis. Federn focused on the concept of ego boundaries and ego-feeling. Psychosis was viewed not as an enrichment or hyperinvestment of the ego at the expense of outside involvement, but rather, as an impoverishment of ego cathexis. In this context, hallucinations and delusions represent lesions or "holes" in the ego itself with the unconscious id breaking through.

Federn's new concept was that the ego was an actual "sensation," which he called ego-feeling. Narcissism, in the form of ego-feeling, joins with emotion in the form of subjective sensation. These early ideas much later served as the nidus for self psychology. Federn believed that one became aware of ego-feeling only when there were disruptions in it. We come back to Amy's mini-idealizations of Dr. Potter. As he provides "support and sustenance," would his absence be felt as a "disruption in ego-feeling?" Amy's need is to fill the narcissistic gap, and thus, she generates a more powerfully sustaining ally—the Potter god. At the same time, Amy puts on her masklike smile; there is something less alive, less genuine about it. As Federn pointed out, object libido and ego libido may function in parallel lines. Feelings of estrangement from external objects may represent a decrease of ego libido rather than an increase in ego libido. And since ego libido (primary narcissism) is responsible for the feeling of aliveness and engagement (continuity, contiguity, and causality), Amy is transiently estranged. As self-esteem goes down, psychosis goes up. But where does affect tie in?

AFFECTS ARE EGO BOUNDARIES IN MOTION

Federn believed that the emotions resulted from intact ego boundaries in motion. Flexible, cohesive ego boundaries equate with good affect tolerance. As self-esteem goes up, affective capacity goes up. And vice versa. Garfield, Rogoff, and Steinberg (1987) conducted a study showing that schizophrenic patients with poor affect recognition also had lower self-esteem than those schizophrenic patients with higher affect recognition capacities. The more you can bear to feel, in general, the better you feel about yourself.

FEELINGS, NARCISSISM, AND ESTRANGEMENT

Amy's clownlike plastic smile was clearly "put on." Potter sensed a distance there. The smile was not real. Yet, later, after Amy had felt understood by Dr. Potter and after she accessed her real feelings by singing, the smile became genuine. It was as though the contact with affect, as facilitated by the doctor, led to a more alive, present, and real communication. Hope, the emotion of volition and narcissism, brought her back in. Hope serves to make contact with the other emotions; it broadens the individual's affective capacity and, thus, the ability to make contact with others. With this renewal, Amy Mills can let the overidealization go; she comes back to what is real.

THE SENSE OF THE REAL

Things are either felt as being a part of us or not a part of us. The discrimination between that which is felt as pertaining to the ego and that which is felt as belonging to the nonego was what Federn called the "sense" of reality—there is no active reality testing here, it is automatic. If something is not experienced as a part of ourselves, then it is "out there"—in the real, outside world. This is how the determination is made. First, there is a sensation. Immediately, we conclude that there is a "nonself" stimulus. Things that go on inside our minds do not produce sensations. Mental contents invested with ego feeling are not normally sensed. If a piece of our own psyche (mental content) is not invested with ego energy, then it *will* be sensed and we will conclude that it is "not self." Therefore, it belongs to the outside world. Thus, if Amy's thoughts or her own words are not imbued with ego libido, then she will experience them as being from outside herself.

For Federn, as for the modern self psychologists, there was a body/mind unity. Federn believed in the subjective and objective nature of the ego—subjectively, it is the "I"; objectively, it is the "self." Federn defined something he called the "middle voice" of the ego, which allows for every ego function, mental and bodily, to carry the primary self-enjoying ego cathexis, the original narcissistic cathexis. External interests are continuously added on top of this primary narcissistic experience. If the narcissistic cathexis is withdrawn or is not supplied in the individual in sufficient quantities then the individual feels a disagreeable change in vitality and self-unity. If the gap gets big enough from these "ego holes," then psychosis sets in. In an effort to patch things together, the patient will use whatever means are available. Hence, the Potter god and clownlike mask that Amy Mills puts on. They have an air of unreality.

AFFECTS AND SELFOBJECTS

A key turning point in the dialogue between Dr. Potter and Amy Mills was in his suggesting that perhaps, he too (like Mrs. Leary), had not fully seen what was going on with the patient. Why bring the discussion back to the relationship at this time?

Dr. Potter has become important to his patient. Again, as Shakespeare suggests, she loves him not for who he is, but for who she is when she is with him. By admiring her skill at having secured the job at Harry's, and by not allowing her to demean her own achievement, Potter reignites an essential part of Amy's inner life—her wish to perform. Her ideal self is a singer, a performer. Dr. Potter serves to rekindle hope, and hope leads her from Harry's to a multitude of inner passions. With an increase in self-esteem, there is a concomitant increase in affective capacity. Dr. Potter fills the gap in "ego feeling."

As mentioned in Chapter 7, Garfield and Havens (1993) suggested that modern psychiatry may be witnessing a shift in theory similar to that seen between Klein and Freud. Freud established the internal agencies of the id, ego, and superego/ego-ideal, and later, Klein peopled them with internal representations of self and others. As Kohut (1971) developed his theory of the self and selfobject, we may now be seeing that the internal structure of the ego-ideal is the correlate ground for the action of selfobjects. If Tony Potter serves as a selfobject for Amy Mills, what exactly does that mean?

In 1971, Kohut began to define the **self-object** in terms of the patient's own experience:

> The small child, for example, invests other people with narcissistic cathexes and thus, experiences them narcissistically, i.e., as selfobjects. The expected control over such (self-object) others is then closer to the concept of the control which a grownup expects to have over his own body and mind than to the concept of the control which he expects to have over others. (p. 27)

Later, Kohut dropped the hyphen in the spelling of selfobject, and thus emphasized the subjective, unifying role that selfobjects play in human experience. Stolorow and Lachmann (1980) further delineated the functional aspect of the selfobject "as a substitute for the missing or defective self-esteem-regulating psychic structure." The self-esteem regulating structure provides "positive affective coloring of the self representation and also maintains the cohesion and stability of the self representation (the structural foundation upon which self-esteem rests)."

In their illustrative article, "The Treatment of Psychotic States," Stolorow and Atwood (Stolorow, Brandchaft, & Atwood, 1987), two creative and radical psychoanalytic theoreticians, describe a self-psychological approach to a young woman, Anna, who suffered from frequent dissolution of her sense of self. Validation of her subjective psychic reality is the prescribed cornerstone of the recovery process from psychosis. They asserted, "What Anna required, at this stage of treatment, was for her analyst to join her as she underwent the oscillations of being and non-being" (p. 166). It was only when the therapist could "decenter" himself from his own need to have the patient be a certain way, that the healing process could begin. Therapists must be open and vulnerable to have their own core ideas about reality challenged. They must be able to get themselves into a position where they can fill the gap. This process, the authors proposed, entails the reestablishment of an archaic selfobject bond between patient and doctor that allows for a firming of the self. The patient gets an early essential need met. In this way, the patient can regain the experience of self in temporal continuity, affective aliveness, and internal cohesiveness.

A whole range of psychotic phenomena, such as Amy Mills's delusional God references or body/face contortions may have new functional psychotherapeutic significance. Here, the selfobject notion may provide clinicians with an important new vantage. These kinds of phenomena tend to emerge **in the context of empathic failure** as experienced by the patient. Whether the empathic failure be that of an idealized therapist who develops a defect, or the kind seen in Amy where a vacation absence combines with a therapeutic misattunement, these psychotic phenomena can best be viewed as intrapsychic procedures functioning to prevent fragmentation. In becoming "reglued" to the emotions and sensations, a selfobject experience takes place. This is reminiscent of the 19th-century descriptive psychiatrists where the concept of splitting of the psychic functions competed with the notion of autism as the main culprit in psychosis. For patients with psychosis, the selfobject function may serve as an antidote for splitting apart.

GRASPING AT EMOTION: JESSE

Jesse had been in treatment with her doctor for over 2 years. She had been labeled as "schizoaffective" because she would become manic and she also had ongoing neologisms and intermittent delusions. She didn't like lithium because she put on weight. Jesse is 56 years old and has two grown children whom she doesn't contact very much because she's ashamed of her financial status. She's living on disability and has been in and out of mental hospitals for over 20 years. She's divorced from Al, but she still has occasional telephone contact with him concerning the kids even though he is remarried. She recalls how she supported Al during his alcoholic days and how she nursed him back to health. Much of Jesse's concerns have to do with men, particularly her famous father. He had obtained custody of Jesse after Jesse's mother had died in a tragic car accident. Unfortunately, Jesse's mom had separated from him just prior to the accident and he was bitter. During the course of treatment, Jesse had remembered many incidents in which her father had been physically abusive to her; as a 2- and 3-year-old, she had been terrified because he would lift her up to the top of a door and let her hang from it and then not help her down. She remembers feeling as if her arms were going to come out of their sockets. He was a tall and big man, who was a powerful businessman in town; he commanded a great deal of respect. She admired him immensely and ardently sought out his love. Yet, his bitterness toward Jesse's dead mother prevailed—since Jesse was the spitting image of her mom, the father treated the daughter very poorly. When he remarried, his new wife resented and scorned her as well.

Jesse took an immediate liking to her new therapist, who seemed to understand her emotions. The fact that Jesse knew she had a million dollars in gold locked in Fort Knox with no way to get at it was sensed as terrible dilemma from the clinician's empathic perspective. Jesse was excited that the therapist did not label her as being "crazy." She felt listened to, and the clinician appreciated Jesse's playfulness and her lovingness.

The therapist suspected that the fact that he was an appreciative male figure was of no small consequence to Jesse's settling down in therapy. He wasn't exactly sure what he meant to her, but he knew he was important to her. When he sprained his ankle during a ski trip, he was somewhat surprised by Jesse's response.

Jesse: Julie, your secretary, told me that you did this to our ankle on your trip.

Th: Yes, that's what happened. How are you (she passes over the therapist's question)?

Jesse: So, how's my ankle (her affect is "blunt," slightly anxious)?

At this point, the therapist is truly confused. He isn't sure if she is referring to the collective ankle she just mentioned or to her own ankle or if she is referring to his ankle. He feels decentered.

Th: Your ankle?

Jesse: (laughs at his confusion) Yes, silly—you are so silly . . .

BECOMING DECENTERED: THE THERAPIST CAN ACCESS NEW EMOTION

Jesse goes on to discuss what has been going on in her life, her new job as a supervisor for a home health care service. She's thinking of trying to buy a used violin—her mother had been a concert violinist and she had tried to play some as a girl, but her father objected and didn't allow it very much because it reminded him of his exwife.

The doctor notices that Jesse is now much more affectively available then she was at the very beginning of the session. Her affection is back. There are no more references to an ankle. He realizes that Jesse accomplished her goal which was to reestablish him as an essential selfobject—she did this through the ambiguous reference to his, her, the collective, ankle. Later when Jesse brings up her exhusband Al and the fact that he's still vulnerable to alcoholism, the therapist seizes the opening.

Th: What does it take to heal these guys? Huh? (Jesse laughs a nervous laugh.)

The therapist's question tied together Jesse's past efforts to offset her father's pain which had been caused by her deceased mother (no fault of her own), her efforts to heal her broken exhusband's alcoholism (no fault of hers) and, in addition, the transference relationship to the therapist, with his injured ankle (no fault of hers). At the same time, the narcissistic gap was still filled; the interpretation was made within the context of the clinician's having made himself available to her.

Th: Were you worried that I would hang you up by your ankles?

Jesse knew the reference to her father because so much time had been spent discussing how her limbs had been almost pulled out by her dad's hanging her from the doorway. It was a "model affect scene" (Lichtenberg, 1989) for Jesse. What became apparent was that she harbored fears about the therapist possibly turning on her, just as she had feared her father. Now she was able to talk about these hidden fears in the context of a secure selfobject transference. Interestingly, the therapist found that "psychotic" expressions (her confusing the ankle) such as the physical boundary confusion seemed to diminish when he came back into empathic connection with her. The therapist could see her reaccess her emotions.

ROCKY

Rocky had broken off treatment with his clinician about a year ago. He didn't completely break things off, but he said that it cost too much money and now that he had tapered himself off the haloperidol and desipramine (and he had been off them for a year and a half), he was doing well. He had a girlfriend, a good consulting job with a software company, and finally his own apartment. He lived a nonmaterialistic lifestyle, and the job didn't pay a large salary.

The patient and psychotherapist had worked together for 3 years. The treatment began after Rocky had suffered from a paranoid period where he thought that John, a colleague in his computer science program, had intentionally conspired to ruin his life by screwing up Rocky's home computer and by turning all of Rocky's friends against him, particularly Rocky's old girlfriend, Gina. The precipitant to Rocky's distress was a confrontation he had with John where Rocky finally stood up for himself. John had the habit of taking Rocky's ideas and presenting them to the computer science faculty as his own. Rocky generally let these events pass by, but he finally decided that it was not right and confronted John in front of two faculty members. John bluffed his way out of the embarrassment but confronted Rocky later. Rocky continued to hold his ground and John began to spread rumors that Rocky was a fraud. Although none of Rocky's friends believed John, Rocky became very insecure and started to defend himself everywhere and protested his innocence. He became extremely anxious, believing that John was ruining him and his credibility.

Although Rocky seemed to rely on the therapist a great deal and seemed to report much of what was going on with him, he also seemed to believe that he had to convince the clinician that he was not crazy.

His symptoms remitted as the therapist empathized with his rage toward John using counterprojective statements. Yet, Rocky still felt that the therapist didn't believe him (and he was right). Rocky discussed his dead father, and he got in touch with how much he missed him. He began to have some affectionate feelings toward the therapist despite the therapist's recalcitrance to fully believe.

When Rocky came back to treatment, the therapist realized that he had missed the boat. He hadn't quite caught on to what Rocky really needed from him. John had disappeared from his life for 2½ years but now was back. When Rocky came back to therapy, he disclosed how important the therapist was to him. The directness and degree of his commitment was impressive. The clinician found himself leaving behind any idea of what was really going on with Rocky. He knew that he wanted to be there for him in the way that Rocky needed.

Rocky went into detail about how John was back and how he himself had forgotten about what had happened. Rocky stated that he had come to believe that there had been something wrong "inside of him" rather than "outside of him." Now he knew that, more than ever, he had to convince others that he was not "crazy" or "paranoid." He feared the therapist really believed that he was paranoid.

Interestingly, 99% of these discussions made perfect sense. The therapist decided, at the risk of entering a "folie à deux," to believe the other 1%. When he did, he was terrified. In fact, he had goose bumps. It reminded him of a John LeCarre novel. He started to feel Rocky's feelings, and they were terribly disconcerting. Once again, by being decentered, the therapist had greater access to affect.

Th: Rocky, I have to tell you that when you came back and told me what was going on with John again, that it scared the hell out of me— **a lot.**

Rocky: That's good—I mean it's not good that you feel that way but I feel that way all the time—my mother doesn't understand at all. She doesn't believe that someone could really do these things— she wants me to say that I'm sick and need medicine—I mean I do need something for this terror and anxiety—I can't function like this—but even more than that, I need to establish my credibility.

That was it. Rocky needed someone to help him feel credible. This was the nature of the narcissistic gap and this was what was preventing him from having a more affectionate attitude toward himself.

Th: What can I do to help?

Rocky: Could you write a list of what you think is good about me? Just the key words?

Th: Sure.

The therapist realized that Rocky needed something concrete that was a statement of someone important to him believing **in** him. As the therapist began to read the list, he realized how much he admired Rocky— his honesty, his articulateness, his creativity, his loyalty, his kindness, his strength. Rocky had reestablished a crucial bond in the therapeutic relationship. John didn't seem like such a big threat anymore. Given the lifelong absence of his father, here was the direct admiration he had been missing from a man.

In summary, clinicians need to recognize the crucial role they play in the recohering of the psychotic patient's psyche. Something is missing that helps hold things together. This is the narcissistic gap to which Benedetti (1987) refers. It may take time to find out exactly what the patient needs from the therapist in terms of a feeling-based relationship. This information is most often gleaned from an understanding of the patient's past and from clues from how the patient relates to the therapist in the here and now (the transference). When the patient needs the therapist in a certain way and when the therapist is attuned to this need, defensive posturing and psychotic phenomena tend to diminish.

Often the patient may press for something that the therapist feels he or she is unable to give. If at that moment, the therapist can decenter and allow him- or herself to consider meeting this need, the demand or request frequently becomes inconsequential because the therapist is able to access new affects that are of central importance to the patient. "Being believed" is often a crucial part of this process because it signals "being believed in," which is essential to a cohesive sense of self. This allows for the patient to believe in him- or herself. This belief posits a "self" in which the individual believes. Now there is a subject self ("I") and an experiencing self ("me"). This reflexivity allows the patient to actively feel and, in addition, to passively feel his or her feelings. Emotion begins to circulate and unbearable affects can begin to be integrated back into the psyche at large. The therapist navigator who is attuned to his or her required role can lend a missing hand, can become a new set of eyes for the patient. And, consequently, the patient, at sea with psychosis, can better act on the natural world and better determine the best routes toward optimal destinations.

9

BEARING
UNBEARABLE AFFECT

BEARING THE UNBEARABLE: JACK BARNES

The sand was unbearably hot, yet Tony refused to get up. His mind said "get up" but his body could not do it. He figured it wouldn't be more than a first-degree sunburn and, in some ways, the relief he felt at having the heat of the sun infuse his exhausted body more than made up for the discomfort of the sand.

Nancy had not been wild about taking vacation in the Caribbean and lying on a beach, yet Tony knew that if he didn't take care of himself and replenish his internal stores, he wouldn't stand a chance upon his return to Boston. The work would eat him up. Was he depressed? No. Was he neurovegetative? Yes. The difference, he concluded was in the will. His will, at this time, was on the side of his psyche. An old saying played over again in his mind: "If you don't bend, you break." As the developmental psychologists noted, one wanted to be stable and flexible rather than rigid and inflexible. Tony had learned that those clinicians who feel that psychotic patients are fragile should be ever aware of how inflexible they are as well. Then again, getting people to change is never an easy proposition. His thoughts were interrupted by a fly that insisted on biting his nose. Now stirred up, Tony figured a walk along the beach was probably a good idea.

How do you tell people about what you do when you work with people in the midst of psychotic storms? Nancy, of course, could see some the effects on him: his mood, his intermittent rantings, his uncontrollable laughing at what would otherwise seem like a horrible situation. Let's face it, he

117

thought, it's a crazy business. Yet, he couldn't remember ever having been as touched by any of his past experiences. Nothing had ever moved him like this work moved him. Nothing had ever challenged him to call on all his internal resources—his own tripartite mind—his thinking, his emotions, his will. And to be allowed into the private home of an individual's heart and mind was a privilege. To bear witness and try to be of some help to a heart, body, and soul in turmoil was why he had wanted to be a physician in the first place.

During these days on the beach, Tony's thoughts frequently went to Jack Barnes. Would he get better? With Amy Mills, Tony could see the forward movement—it didn't matter to him that she wasn't "cured" or "normal." Who ever was? But after 1½ years, Tony couldn't see any movement with Jack. Where would change show itself? What if there wasn't any change? Do you give up? Are you "required" to give up? Had Jack given up? Does a person have to "give up" before he or she can "get"? This seemed too Zen-like for a vacation, so he decided to drop it. The freedom to not think was a requirement for mental health. Some of his patients with catatonia were not so lucky—they were automatically obedient, even to their own thoughts. Prisoners of the immediate experience. For now, Tony would rest.

Interestingly, some answers started to appear upon his return. Even though Jack had left the hospital and was in a halfway house, his emotional life was still "blunted." That is to say that Jack didn't show emotion—not on his face, not in the tone of his voice, not in his words. He didn't blush, didn't scream and didn't talk about feeling blue. Yet, Tony knew that emotion, the basis of life, must be somewhere there.

Potter: Hi, Jack. Nice to see you. How's the last two weeks been?

Jack: (glancing at Tony) Fine. I did all my chores.

Potter: Not exactly a vacation, huh?

Jack: No (long silence). Did you get that belt on your vacation?

Potter: (somewhat startled that Jack had noticed) Yeah, I did. What do you think?

Jack: It's nice. It's OK.

Potter: You figure it'll keep my pants up and shirt tucked in?

Jack: (chuckles) Yeah (long silence).

The session continued in spurts. It wasn't until the very end, when Jack was leaving Tony's office that Tony noticed that Jack was wearing a red and blue plaid flannel shirt, similar to the kind that Tony often wore. As Jack was walking out, Tony spontaneously added:

Potter: Hey, nice shirt. Where'd you get it?

Jack: At the Coop (Jack walked off). [The Harvard Coop is a cooperative department store in Cambridge, MA.]

It was then that Tony realized that perhaps they had more in common than he had realized. Jack's shirt was not only similar to Tony's kind but it was colorful as well. His clothes before had been brown or gray or washed-out colors. There was movement in the color of Jack's new shirt.

Tony used this discovery to broaden and deepen his relationship with Jack. He began to use Jack as a clothes consultant. When Tony got new shoes, he asked Jack what Jack thought about them. Were penny loafers too casual for a psychiatry resident or did Jack think it was OK? Jack got a kick out of Tony's seeking out his opinion and spontaneously offered up comments, most of which were supportive. Tony noticed that Jack continued to come in with a greater variety of shirts, but what impressed Tony the most was the spontaneity of communication that Jack evinced. The two of them were "clicking" much better together. Their spontaneous affectivity was meeting at the boundary land of their appearances.   ◆

CHANGES IN AFFECT

As Semrad and Van Buskirk (1969) commented:

> Before schizophrenia becomes chronic schizophrenia, a way of life, the ego fights to regain reality in preference to pursuing the self-consoling activity of psychotic transformation . . . the acute patient tends to a restitutive posture even in his language, symbols, and symptoms . . . The healthy capacity to feel what there is to be felt, to think what there is to be thought, and to circulate these through one's total experience is replaced by cautious, erratic phrases and private language. . . . Bizarre irrelevancies or cryptic neologisms often prove to be verbal expressions of intolerable body sensations.
>
> The chronic schizophrenic person finds himself at an impasse in the matter of communication. He does not want to know. He does not want to think about the unbearable affect-laden issues . . . and he relentlessly denies the potential of others to help. The more chronic the clinical condition, the more solidified the stance. . . . (p. 25)

Perhaps, Dr. Potter had been searching too far to see how Jack Barnes had started to change. To get the big picture, clinicians must first see what's directly in front of their noses. This is an easy error to make. Dr. Potter's reflections on the beach about flexibility and stability could actually be seen in Barnes's behavior. Barnes was not walking around the streets talking to parking meters, he was not erratically grimacing, he was not "unstable." The rigidity had started to develop some "give." Jack would show up for his therapy appointments, and every now and then he would initiate the conversation.

However, in the arena of Jack Barnes's emotional life, Dr. Potter had missed the boat. It was not just an identification with the type of shirt his therapist wore that was a signal of increased affectivity, but it was the color, too. What had been unbearable and turned inward was now becoming more tolerable and displayed in color. Mobilized emotion begins to bring life back to the human container. Affects are the bonds of the human psyche. To aid in the recovery process, to assist as a "lost mind" finds itself, a psychological being is required, a human container, circulator and bearer of affect. The therapeutic relationship makes that being possible. In wondering about the meaning of the similarity between Jack Barnes's plaid shirt and Dr. Potter's, we come back to the experienced Italian psychoanalyst, Benedetti (1987):

> I formulate (it) as the attempt at the "overinclusion" of the therapist in the schizophrenic symbol. I am bold enough to conceptualize it as an integrating instrument of psychotherapy. Overinclusion of the therapist within the structure of the schizophrenic symbol may act as a yeast that transforms that autistic structure into a communicative one and that prepares a normal psychological introjection, which presupposes, of course, a normal integration of the patient's ego. It is a way of coming near the patient without exposing him to the danger of an "implosion," without stripping away from him those defenses which are necessary to him . . . (pp. 62–63)

By "overinclusion of the therapist within the schizophrenic symbol," Benedetti can be seen to touch on the patient's making contact inside him- or herself, with the emotional life of the therapist.

AN ANALOGY: THE ACUTE ABDOMEN

A young man comes into the emergency room with acute abdominal pain. The surgeon is called in. There is no diagnosis yet; there can be no treatment. Some kind of therapeutic relationship must take shape. Questions are asked, the history is taken. The surgeon moves to examine the patient. The patient lays down, supine, on the table. The surgeon begins to feel, to palpate the belly. There is significant guarding, thus, the approach must be gentle. Although the disease process lays deep below the surface, the healing process begins at the periphery. It begins with the surgeon making contact. It is not just feeling the patient's pain; the surgeon needs the patient to feel the surgeon's fingers: "When I press here, what do you feel?"

Now the patient, in feeling the contact from the surgeon's hands, can feel his own pain. This is the secret to the "laying on of hands."

For Jack Barnes, it is more important that he make contact with Dr. Potter than that Dr. Potter make contact with him. Yet, to be available and accessible and to be at a place where it is possible for the patient to psychologically touch you, is not easy. It has always been a given that the human interface is an essential ingredient of the therapeutic process. The patient needs to interact with a "warm body." By "warm," people really mean "emotional." Making contact with the emotional life of the clinician stimulates the psychotic patient's own inner emotional life. If there is inner disorganization and no experience of being, then coming in contact with the doctor's emotional being in a safe way is an essential first step. For Jack Barnes, "The clothes make the man." In fact, the emotion of the psychiatrist is contacted as Jack wears his colors.

THE ALLIANCE IS THERAPEUTIC

Gutheil and Havens (1979) closely examined the concept of therapeutic alliance and proposed several different types of alliances. First, there is the "rational" alliance. Here, as Sterba (1934), Zetzel (1970), and Greenson (1965) point out, the doctor and the patient join together to work for a common cause. Most notably, the military connotation of the term "alliance" implies that the healthy part of the therapist works with the healthy part of the patient to overcome the enemy—in the medical setting—the illness.

The second type of alliance they describe is the "irrational" alliance. Here, unconscious wishes and desires of the patient seek a possible ally in the therapist. This is also referred to as a positive transference—indeed, Gutheil and Havens stress that transference and alliance are not always altogether separable. "If you resemble someone I have really liked, then you will find it much easier to work with me."

The third alliance they describe is the "narcissistic" alliance where, in fact, no real collaboration exists. Here the therapist is an unwitting piece of the patient's missing puzzle. The patient might be heard to say, "I've been looking for you all along and didn't even know it." This is an alliance through selfobject, as Kohut described. It is "irrational" but it is more. Gutheil and Havens (1979) quote a prominent Boston analyst, Robert Mehlman (1976):

> The patient's initial comfort or fright can be said to be dependent upon a variety of inarticulate factors to which the successful practitioner intuitively

responds. He does a series of things that can be summed up by saying that he determines what the affective locus of immediate narcissistic crisis or problem is, addresses himself to it, intuitively or cognitively, and in the process avoids adding to the fright and actually "diminishes" it sufficiently to allow the patient to include him "irrationally" as part of the adaptive-defensive system already operating. (Gutheil & Havens, 1979, p. 471)

What we see here is an understanding of the therapeutic relationship from the clinician's point of view. As the theory comes closer to the patient, the patient's unbearable affective state becomes the focus. Effective psychotherapy—even at the outset—requires making the unbearable more bearable. Some sort of entity is necessary to contain this process—to allow this metabolism to take place. As Dr. Potter failed to recognize, the most salient progress that Jack Barnes had made was in the formation of that third entity—the therapeutic relationship.

PRELUDE TO CONTACT

How did Dr. Potter and Jack Barnes arrive at a therapeutic relationship? One self was and one self wasn't. Does the therapist speak to a "self to be?" Or must something else take place? In his initial efforts to meet with Jack, Dr. Potter encountered some characteristic difficulties, such as Jack not showing up for appointments or being quite late. It wasn't just Potter's sheer effort and dependability that allowed a relationship to emerge, but rather, some kind of communication occurred. Semrad and Van Buskirk (1969); Sullivan (1956); Benedetti (1987); and others have pointed to working within the psychotic symptoms as being a necessary first step in allowing the patient to make contact with the doctor. To return to the surgical analogy, contact is made at the periphery. The doctor works emotionally, with empathy, to "feel" his or her way into the patient's dilemma, to understand the painful affects that the psychotic symptoms attempt to avoid. Yet, the symptoms are also a communication of the avoided "feeling-toned complex." Through these maneuvers, the doctor feels the patient's psychological belly. The kind of contact required for a therapeutic alliance is invisible, yet absolutely essential. Despite the guarding, the patient must feel himself as he feels the psychological hands of the doctor pressing first on one side and then on the other. The signals the patient emits, the noises, the sounds, the unusual communications are all part of the development of the therapeutic relationship. When we answer back, make explanations or interpretations, the internal emotions and sensations of the patient begin to move; they begin to circulate.

AFFECTIVITY AND SELF-SECURITY IN SCHIZOPHRENIA

The founder of the interpersonal approach to psychosis, Harry Stack Sullivan (1956) asked:

> What then does one do? One has to structure the relationship with the schizophrenic by, first, avoiding any avoidable, foreseeable disturbance of the patient's security . . . an exquisite care in avoiding unnecessary bad jolts . . . will at least give you a good chance to maintain communications. This good chance at communicating with the schizophrenic implies, by my definition, that the precise meanings of words in your mind and in the patient's mind are probably by no means identical . . . . (p. 367)

Initial attention to self-esteem, self-regard, and self-confidence help put the therapeutic alliance on good footing. With a sense that he or she is already doing a reasonable job given the storms at hand, the psychotic patient can become less defensive. There is more room to feel, sense, and process internal information. This is the important notion that as security and self-esteem go up, affectivity goes up as well. Sullivan reminds us that the gentle psychological probing, the communication with what is provided, must not jolt the patient. For the surgeon, the patient must believe that no harm will come from the exam. The sensation of being touched must not be overwhelming in order for the therapeutic alliance to materialize. For the psychotic patient, attempts at communication must be met with a responsivity that allows for internal sensation and affect to be elicited without too much fear.

As a superb student of infants, Daniel Stern (1977), in his book *The First Relationship,* has provided a detailed account of how the infant contacts his or her mother and how affective attunement concurrently takes shape. To a certain extent, the same is true in the therapeutic relationship between a psychotic patient and the clinician. As the infant is touched and engaged in an empathically attuned way, the infant comes to psychological life, through the vehicle of this first relationship. As Dr. Potter discovered in his therapy with Jack Barnes, the therapeutic relationship is often invisible, yet it can be seen in its effect on both the doctor and the patient. One of its most important characteristics is "therapeutic momentum."

AFFECT AND THERAPEUTIC MOMENTUM

As Jack Barnes comes to life in his contact with Dr. Potter, his reality changes color. Normal language reflects the close connection between color and mood as well. "I'm blue" is the saying. Or "she's beet red" with embarrassment. And "he's green" with envy. Within the life of the therapeutic relationship, Jack Barnes' psychotic experience now has a place to change. The regularity of meetings, the productivity of speech, the ongoing presence in Dr. Potter's mental life—all speak to **movement** in therapy. These all speak to a pace and to a force for change that can be called "therapeutic momentum."

As the treatment establishes a pace, there are many potential indications that the patient's affects are now beginning to circulate. We are taken back to Federn's understandings of ego boundaries in motion; emotionality is the result. In a fascinating way, the converse is also true; as emotionality stirs, the patient becomes more integrated. A colorful and graphic example of this is in Benedetti's patients' paintings. At each stage of their illness and treatment/recovery, Benedetti (1987) had his patients paint pictures of what was occurring in their inner life. What is most apparent is the change in size and color of internal negative elements, and the appearance, shape and color of emerging internal positive elements. As with Jack's clothes, the paintings were manifestations of not just what was happening inside a patient's psychic life, but within the therapeutic vehicle of the alliance as well. As the alliance takes on momentum, affect has both a home and a destination.

TOLERANCE

As intolerable affect becomes tolerable, as therapeutic momentum moves the therapeutic relationship forward, the pain of the unusual transforms itself into a degree of comfort with the familiar. It is not that there are no new discoveries to be made, but rather that exploration is now safe. The words and actions of the world around become the items of commerce, not the horrors of assault. A new tolerance develops.

As recovery from psychosis takes place, emotion combines more easily with the other two parts of the tripartite mind, cognition and the will. No longer must one's own thoughts be interpreted in a rigid fashion. Now, possibilities exist and there is less pressure to foreclose on alternatives. It is safe to come out from hiding; it is OK to share the boat with the therapist crewmate, especially within the therapeutic relationship. Autism undergoes a metamorphosis, into awkward shyness.

For Jack Barnes, this metamorphosis means he can now take a risk. He can show up. He can try on a new look. The will is summoned forth, and assertiveness bears witness to the emergence of hope. Yet, the patient can't do it alone; in making unbearable affect more bearable, the doctor must be able to tolerate and convey the idea that the patient can leave psychosis behind.

IS SALLY SAFE?

The therapist had been working with Sally for 4 years. For the first 3 years, she was seen two or three times a week. Sally came from a middle-class Jewish family and she had been married twice. During a cocaine-induced manic episode at the age of 37, she had left her second husband. She was given safe harbor by a young Catholic man from work. Sally worked as the office manager of a small architectural design firm. Her boyfriend, Bob, was a draftsman there. He was infatuated with her—she was fun, thoughtful, loving, and direct. She had slept with him in the midst of all the turmoil. Before she came for outpatient treatment, she had been given lithium, stelazine, and benztropine. Although she had never been approached or bothered by anyone who ever sold her drugs, she was terrified that drug dealers were going to kill her. She believed that people on the street were watching her movements and might try to attack her in her apartment.

As the work progressed, the clinician learned more about the details of Sally's marriages. Her first husband had been fun but not trustworthy. He cheated on her and she ignored a plethora of telltale signs until he finally left her. Interestingly, she appeared to have had a mild depressive episode just after she was engaged to him. Two years after her divorce, she married a computer analyst. He was emminently trustworthy, but he treated her like a child, constantly telling her that her fun-loving nature was a sign of irresponsibility. They had no children. Two years into the marriage, she began using cocaine on an intermittent basis. She continued to use cocaine sporadically until her recent affair and hospitalization.

The therapist met Sally's family early on in the treatment. As the "baby" of the family, she was both ignored and superficially admired for her beauty and adventurous spirit. Sally settled into a routine of meeting with the therapist and the intensity of her persecutory fears diminished over the first two months. The therapist kept Sally's potential projections off of her through counterprojective statements and focused on buttressing Sally's self-esteem through "given" and performative statements. As the clinician worked with her, she resisted the idea that her family had been emotionally unresponsive to her and that their devaluation and admiration both missed the point—the point being her. The therapist was impressed with how Sally was tuned into her, the therapist, and everyone else. Yet, other than some distress over her job or problems with her new boyfriend, she displayed little emotion. She was friendly, social, and interactive, but there was little movement in the underlying fear or other emotions inside her.

Using Semrad's tour of the body, the clinician came to understand that her fear was mainly in her chest and that it was like a tightness. Sally would want to bolt out of her boyfriend's house or a friend's apartment. She couldn't pinpoint the first time she had ever felt this tightness-in-her-chest fear, but she thought it wasn't until after her adolescence. Quickly, she picked up on the therapist's style and focus on her and, on occasion, she teased the therapist about it. "What about you?" she wanted to know.

The clinician wasn't sure how much self-disclosure might be helpful. Sally wanted to know what the therapist would do in her situation. When it was gracefully suggested that Sally was in a tough position, Sally pressed further. "What would you do? Would you get your own apartment? Would you leave Bob to have time to work out the prior marriages on your own and risk losing him? Or would you continue along?" Here, Sally was looking to make contact with the therapist. Knowing how difficult making plans is for those who are caught by persecutory fears, Sally's clinician went through the alternatives with her, but even that didn't quite do the trick. Originally, Sally had been pressured by her family to see the therapist on a regular basis. Over the preceding year, she had insisted on coming off the medication and had no recurrence of major illness. Occasional fear episodes still occurred, but they were minor. She decided to take a break from treatment.

Six months later, Sally called back and said she needed to see the therapist, that her paranoia had come back. She related that she felt that Bob was from a different culture—he loved her and she loved him and they had a wonderful time together, but he wasn't Jewish. She reported increasing episodes of "paranoia," and the clinician wondered if these were panic attacks—yet, they didn't really fit the description. In addition, there was no simple dynamic equation where she was annoyed or humiliated or conflicted and then her symptoms would emerge. As Sally reentered treatment in this 4th year, she seemed to take charge of her life more. Now, Sally was back in treatment because she wanted it, not because her family was pressing her. She had even asked for a raise at work. She wanted to come weekly and pay for it herself without family assistance.

After a month or so, the paranoid episodes diminished markedly and her therapist knew that reestablishment of the therapeutic alliance was a major factor in helping her bear her fear. Odd things began to show themselves in the treatment. Sally would sit in different chairs in the consulting room. For a long while, she chose the one that her mother had sat in when the family had come in for an early session. She also bought a new handbag that was similar to the one that her mother had. But within 2 months she abandoned the chair and handbag. They weren't for her, she said. Although Sally did not adopt the therapist's skirt, blouse, and sweater attire, she did assume the same calm air that was part of the therapist's demeanor. The therapist noticed that Sally was also trying on different styles of dress. Some were "little-girl styles" with frills and ruffles. Some were sleek and sexy and reminiscent of the 1920 flapper era. There was an outfit for boating with a short sweater and pants that were three-quarter length. There was a lot of movement in style and color and age-appropriateness.

When Sally pressed about what the therapist had done in college—what her major was, what her social life was like—the therapist began to give her more information. It almost didn't seem to matter to her what the specific response was, and the clinician noticed that often Sally wouldn't remember what had been said a month or two earlier. It occupied very little of the treatment, but the specific responsivity was clearly important to the patient.

Most notably, it was a time of great disclosure for Sally in the therapy. She talked a great deal about her relationship with her mother and how she was upset that her mom never interacted with Sally's friends. Her mom seemed to want to be alone, to read, to think. Her dad was a caring fellow who was absorbed by his work as a tax attorney. When he was home, he was fun, attentive, and available but those were the rare times. It was learned that few of her family members really knew her deeply. They all had their prototypic image of Sally and that was it.

As her inner emotions began to circulate more freely, not only did her dress and style change frequently, but her fear became more bearable. She began to generate new hypotheses about why she might get fearful in the situations in which the episodes occurred. She was a real working partner in the treatment, and the therapist let her know that her participation was crucial and appreciated. The alliance deepened, and the therapist believed that a "mirroring" (Kohut, 1971) selfobject transference was helping to fill Sally's narcissistic gap.

Sally came to feel that her paranoid episodes occurred when she had a preference or wish for herself, yet didn't feel free to express it. This would heighten if she believed she had given some signal of her wishes and that there was no response on the part of the important other. She told of several occurrences with Bob and her sister and with waiters at restaurants where there was no acknowledgment of her position. Then the paranoia would set in. At these times in the sessions, Sally would, concurrently, probe the therapist further about herself. It was brought up to her that she needed to have some kind of response and interaction from the therapist, rather than dealing with a woman who would hide her nose in some psychiatric book or approach. Sally became more open to these kinds of transference interpretations and comparisons to her relationship with her mother.

Yet, for Sally to mobilize and circulate her affects, she needed to make contact with the emotional life of the psychotherapist. The therapist wondered if the real reason Sally had broken off treatment for the 6-month block was that she had been frustrated in not being able to make some kind of connection to the clinician's own internal emotional life. Once that happened, then Sally's own affects were set in motion, the therapeutic alliance took on momentum, and what was unbearable affect was now brought under joint custody. Psychotic storms were avoided as the two partners maneuvered their way through spells of mild turbulence.

SECTION III

A LIFE'S WORK: STAYING OUT OF PSYCHOSIS

10
PUTTING EMOTION IN PERSPECTIVE

ENLISTING OTHERS: AMY MILLS

Three years had passed since Tony Potter graduated from his psychiatry residency at Mount Sinai Hospital in Boston. He continued to work with Amy Mills for two of those years, until Amy had moved down to Manhattan to live with an old friend from high school. Amy had obtained a job behind the ticket window of a small, off-Broadway theater, and although it barely paid for her rent and utilities, she sounded pretty happy. She wrote to Tony weekly for the first 6 months and he would write her back a brief note, most of the time. After that, he would hear from her every couple of months. It was always good to hear from her.

Tony wondered about the fact that they had not had a "proper" termination to the therapy. He had taken a job at the state hospital affiliated with the medical school, and he had a small private practice. Amy fit into neither of those modes and Tony figured that part of her leaving was that she didn't want treatment from him for free or near free. She had, perhaps, refound her pride. The envy of her sister toward her and the guilt and anger that she felt in return had been dealt with in the course of their 4 years together and the immediacy and intensity of those affects had receded. Also, it seemed that she had regained some of her old confidence. He knew that the rekindling of old friendships and her return to be near the theater were good signs. She was still on the lithium and Tony had arranged for a psychiatrist in Manhattan to be available for her medication every couple of months. Amy wrote about taking classes from a master

131

teacher at the theater. This was an older woman whom Amy respected a great deal and they seemed to have an affinity toward each other. Amy was able to take lessons in exchange for working at the theater. It was satisfying to Tony that Amy had been able to "enlist" people into her life who would be good to her and for her.

In Search of Emotional Stability: Arnie Davis

The idea of "enlisting" helpful others as being a signpost of recovery from psychosis was much on Tony's mind as he started working with Arnie Davis. Arnie had previously been given a diagnosis of bipolar affective disorder with psychotic features. Arnie had come into Mount Sinai toward the end of Tony's residency and had now been in treatment for 3½ years. Their first meeting had made a lasting impression on the, then, senior resident. Arnie had been discharged and showed up at Tony's outpatient intake clinic.

Arnie: So, you're Dr. Tiger, huh?

(Tony had been teased as a kid about being "Tony the Tiger"—from the cereal box—and it was his first association but he knew enough not to jump to conclusions.)

I see, I'm supposed to call you Dr. Potter even though you're really Dr. Tiger. What have you got against cats anyway? They're much more reliable than humans. You are Tony the Tiger, right?

Potter: (finally allows himself to laugh) You figure I'm just like Tony the Tiger, huh? Looks tough but you know he's a pussycat.

Arnie: (chuckles) Yes, he is a pussycat. Some of my best friends are pussycats—want to see (Arnie pulls out pictures of his cats at home)?

Potter: (taking a long careful look) Is this one a Persian?

Arnie: Good Heavens, no. Don't you know anything? You really need to learn much more about cats. That's a tabby.

(Tony had a feeling that he was at the beginning of a feline education.)

I do think that you are a cat, a large cat (gives Tony a big grin).

Potter: What makes me a large cat?

Arnie: You'll see. You have claws and you hiss (hisses). (Long pause) Did I show you my poem for Mother's Day?

Potter: No.

Arnie: Mothers are the world's most important people. They take care when no one else will. Mothers do the dishes and wash the clothes. They clean the house and cook the meals. They take care of you when you are sick. None of us would be here if it wasn't for Mothers.

Potter: (struck by the childlike quality of this poem following the patient's exhibition of a brief period of delusional perception) Definitely a poem for Mother's Day.

Arnie: I gotta go. I'll see you next week.

Recruitment of a Psychiatrist

Arnie Davis was living with a quiet, older woman in a small two-bedroom apartment. He and his friend, Ethyl, did not have a romantic relationship, but they had been friends and roommates for almost 15 years. Ethyl worked as the office manager of a printing press, and Arnie, on disability, took care of the home front.

The next few weeks were somewhat turbulent as Arnie was uncertain whether Dr. Potter would recognize him for more than a chronic mental patient. If Tony asked which prior medications had been helpful, Arnie would abruptly stand up, point his finger at Tony, and say "You're a stupid man." When Tony called him the next day to try to repair the new alliance, he discovered that Arnie had thrown some crystal glasses at the wall and shattered them. Yet, he let Tony know that he had taken careful aim to avoid injuring his cats in any way. Ethyl had been at work. These follow-up phone calls seemed to do the trick. Arnie was reassured that Dr. Potter was not "blowing him off" and the therapy continued.

For most of his adult life, unlike now, Arnie had been in intense relationships with women. Almost invariably, the ending would be stormy and Arnie would get depressed, become delusional that he was evil and that there was an evil force inside him, and he would cut himself. This pattern began at the age of 18 years, when he stabbed himself in the stomach ("It felt like there was a knot, a big ball in there that I needed to cut out"). He would be hospitalized for the "schizophrenic" episodes four or five times a year. Five years ago, he had been rediagnosed as having bipolar affective disorder, and even with his current stable relationship with Ethyl, he still was hospitalized about twice a year.

Most of his recent hospitalization occurred either because Arnie felt that someone had been condescending toward him or because he felt accused of not doing something that he was supposed to be doing. For example, Arnie volunteered at a nearby church soup kitchen. When the kitchen manager would comment that the stove should be cleaner, Arnie would get furious. He felt that the manager did nothing and lorded his power over all who worked there. In addition, Arnie worked extremely hard and diligently at almost everything he did and, thus, he felt totally unrecognized and unappreciated. He would become angry, then enraged, and then delusional. Then he would get hospitalized. He had refused to take lithium or any of the anticonvulsants but always agreed to take chlorpromazine. These "psychotic" episodes would consist of his believing that people were plotting against him, accusing him of being perverted, and trying to "pin things on me." After he was in the hospital for a few days, even without medication, the delusions would remit and he'd return home to Ethyl.

Antecedents to Anger

Arnie's father, John Davis, had been a construction worker; he drank heavily. He was a big man and, when drunk, mercilessly beat Arnie's two older brothers. When the older boys were big enough to fend off dad and Arnie was no longer a toddler, his brothers would sacrifice him to the old man's drunken abuse. They'd hold him while the father would beat him. It was a madhouse. The parents would fight "like cats and dogs," and Arnie remembered the coal stove being overturned as his mother threw plates at his father. He remembered being hit by some of the burning coals and ash. Tony could see, in Arnie's throwing the crystal glasses at the wall, how the past action, when coupled with the feeling tone of anger, repeated itself in the present.

Things went from bad to worse in Arnie's early life. A little sister was born. Long-awaited by the mother, baby Carol not only was given protection from the family fury but was catered to in every way by the parents. Here were the seeds of Arnie's feeling that it was likely that he would be treated unfairly. There was no maternal protection for him. The resentment poured fuel on the fire of his beatings. Just when he was big enough to get away from the fray and get up from down under, the family fell apart. Arnie was 8 years old. He moved in for 6 months with his dad and one brother and then, for 9 months with his mother. Child Protective Services took him away from them altogether and put him in an orphanage. Unfortunately, there was so little supervision and care at the orphanage that Arnie was left to the whim of the older kids, who were not that nice. After 3 years of being bounced around, he went back to live with his mother where he completed high school.

As Tony got the details of Arnie's life, the 60-year-old seemed to settle down. He began to acknowledge unbearable affect. He admitted that he was angry at the soup kitchen supervisors, "damn angry." During the first year of treatment, Arnie was psychiatrically hospitalized only once. Arnie had been on the medical service for glaucoma and when he returned to outpatient treatment, Tony inquired as to whether Arnie had felt bad that Tony hadn't visited. Arnie said "no." Tony said, "Well, some flowers and a card might have been a decent thing to do." At that point, Arnie abruptly stood up and walked out. Tony got a call the next day from Arnie. Arnie felt he needed to be hospitalized. He was confused and felt suicidal. It was a brief, 3-day hospitalization where the patient was restarted on chlorpromazine (he wouldn't accept any other medication). A week after that, Arnie stated that he felt he could get along without the medicine. Months later, he told

Tony that he had been "pissed off" that Tony had felt that Arnie would want Tony to be sexually "turned on" to him; that he would somehow want Tony to send him flowers like "a boyfriend would send to a girlfriend." After Tony clarified that had not been his intent at all, Arnie seemed much more relaxed. It would have been easy to frame this as homosexual panic, but Tony erred on the side of self-esteem. Arnie did not want to be considered weak and helpless, especially by Tony.

Anger and the Beast

When Arnie would get "pissed off," his anger showed itself in many forms. Along with the suspicions, confusion, and delusional perception of Tony as the Tiger, Arnie would intermittently "feel" himself to be the "Beast." This was a private experience, which he rarely discussed with Ethyl. It was most noticeable to him when he worked at his computer. He kept a series of files that were his conversations with the Beast. Occasionally, while writing as the Beast, Arnie felt that he had fangs and that droplets of blood were dripping from the fangs into his mouth. He could taste it. Here was another delusional perception. Did this represent some kind of partial complex seizure activity in the temporal lobes or were they dealing with two different affect states—one wanting vengeance and the other ruled by guilt?

Tony came to know other ways in which the Beast was a part of Arnie's life. Arnie and Ethyl had four cats. Tony the Tiger was brought into the fold as a "friend of the family." At a few points during the treatment, Arnie would refer to the cats as his children. Certainly, Tony was of the right age to be Arnie's son. A father-son dyad again. Beast, cat or kitten? Tony wondered. With the tremendous amount of injury that Arnie had suffered at his father's hands, Tony became aware of the contours of the narcissistic gap that needed to be filled.

As they traced out the historical roots of his strict Catholic upbringing, Tony began to realize that here was a fellow who had hired himself a psychotherapist. There was the expectation that Tony would "do his job." In this case, the job was to help Arnie acknowledge, bear, and put into perspective this terrible anger and guilt that led Arnie into episodes of psychosis and kept him from a more successful life. Thus, enlistment subserved the function of taming the Beast and emboldening the Martyr.

Some Special Somatic Phenomena

As the therapeutic alliance became deeper and richer and a therapeutic momentum took hold, Tony became aware of some interesting countertransference phenomena. From time to time, Arnie would focus on specific physical ailments in specific body parts. Almost without exception, Arnie would bring these up at times when Tony was having some kind of minor physical problem in the exact same body part. Many years after his having met Andrew Stevens in New York, Tony made a successful marathon attempt. His interest in psychosis lasted much longer than did his running knees. They were a mess. At times they would give him a good deal of stiffness and pain. At those times when Tony was suffering silently, Arnie would invariably mention difficulty that he was having with his hips. No doubt they both had arthritis. Yet, it was almost as though Tony's pain was showing up in Arnie's hips. It wasn't that Arnie wasn't entitled to his own pain, it was just that Arnie never complained about it except for those times when Tony, himself, was uncomfortable.

At first, Tony wondered whether or not Arnie was attempting, transferentially, to repair his pseudoparent to a state of good health by sharing this burden of pain. Tony would then be a fully available therapist once again. But after Tony was having trouble getting the right contact lens prescription and almost simultaneously, Arnie announced that he needed glaucoma treatment, Tony began to ponder what these "coincidents" were really all about. Certainly, the patient needed to talk about all aspects of his feeling experience. Was there some kind of mutual identification going on? These somatic mergers had occurred seven or eight times. Was he simply noticing his own bodily experiences because Arnie was cuing him to do so in some fashion? Tony knew that these experiences, though confusing, were not negative. Some kind of communication was taking place. He had been through similar "alter ego" experiences before. He also knew he was not exploiting Arnie to bear his bodily discomforts. It did seem that the threat of Tony's being unavailable either by being out sick or because of a hospital staff meeting would induce these phenomena. As Tony reviewed his notes on the sessions, he discovered that these experiences also followed sessions where he had been off track in his interpretations. Thus, the somatic ties might represent a response to empathic failure as well as an attempt to reestablish empathic connection. Here Tony's body was being enlisted in the process of bearing affect when his mind was not able to do the trick.

Becoming Assertive

In this latter part of treatment, Arnie became progressively more assertive. Instead of "getting mad, I get even." Arnie no longer allowed the soup kitchen supervisors to walk over him. In fact, he submitted his resignation. He decided that he wanted to live more "in the real world." He began to frequent computer stores and struck up friendly relationships with some of the guys who worked on the motherboards. He communicated by modem and fax with the software technical advisors. Tony noticed that Arnie's clothes were changing as well. Instead of wearing ill-fitting institutional garb, Arnie began to wear Eddie Bauer outer wear. Emotion was more fully coordinated on the outside as well as the inside. When hit by a nearly blind

80-year-old driver, Arnie sued the insurance company. He gave the money to Ethyl who had supported him through the years and to whom he "owed more than money." When public aid threatened to cancel his benefits because of the money he received from the accident, he threatened to sue them also. He was proud and pleased when they backed off.

As Arnie became more assertive, the Beast moved to the background. Would Tony miss the Beast? Again, psychosis was more dramatic but Tony took satisfaction in the middle ground. The Martyr of guilt would no longer threaten his patient in such a precarious way as when Arnie had slashed his own throat in the past. ✦

BEING ENLISTED: ASSISTING THE RECOVERY FROM PSYCHOSIS

The first contact between Dr. Potter and Arnie Davis established a therapeutic alliance around associations to the clinician's name ("Tony the Tiger") and the patient's need for cats in his life. This was akin to the "irrational/narcissistic" alliance of Gutheil and Havens (1979); Kohut's (1971) selfobject transference is, perhaps, even a better description. Yet, there was more here. Mr. Davis's life had, in fact, been settling down for the past 15 years vis-à-vis his stable relationship with his companion, Ethyl. In this light, Dr. Potter was another enlistee of Arnie Davis. The turbulent beginning of a treatment with a psychotic patient who has been in treatment before is not uncommon and can be considered to be a "test." Could this be a second stable individual who Arnie Martin would find helpful?

This process of enlistment is a crucial landmark in the recovery process from psychosis. Amy Mills' reconnection with her old high school friend as a roommate is a good example of this process. Her seeking out a mentor-teacher at the theater is further evidence of the establishment of a new external milieu that mirrors the internal change. A renewed ego-ideal manifests itself in these relationships. And as Garfield and Havens (1993) suggested, selfobjects may inhabit the ego-ideal in a fashion similar to the way in which self and object representations have been seen to inhabit the psychic agencies of id, ego, and superego.

These key selfobject relationships play a central role in providing an atmosphere where difficult affects can be constructively absorbed. Recall the "high EE" (expressed emotion) ratings of the families within which schizophrenic patients would commonly relapse. By high EE, Wynne and Singer (1963) were referring to interpersonal environments wherein the patient was criticized. Enlistment as a part of the recovery process is the exact opposite. Gradually, the patient assembles a network that is admiring, not critical. These networks help him or her "acknowledge, bear, and put into perspective" previously intolerable emotions. The recovery process now takes on a life of its own.

DR. POTTER'S ROLE WITH ARNIE DAVIS

Ever mindful of the narcissistic gap as well as Arnie Davis's need to temper his anger, Dr. Potter embarked on a process of helping the patient to acknowledge and discover the delusional, physical, and cognitive manifestations of his anger. They learned that the anger made him confused. Harold Searles (1965), the Washington, DC, psychoanalyst who wrote extensively about psychotherapy with psychotic patients, described this very sequence in his paper "Concerning a Psychodynamic Function of Perplexity, Confusion, Suspicion and Related Mental States." In labeling the Beast as being "angry" and in labeling his being accused of inadequacy as generating "guilt," Dr. Potter could establish a new language, a new affective lexicon, within the therapeutic alliance. The delusional suspicions could be understood as making him feel "harassed"—then, "angry." The "agitated" feeling he got with his volunteer supervisor could be labeled as a "guilty" feeling. The primary process may continue along in parallel with secondary process but the patient is able to communicate with a consensual, social, secondary process vocabulary.

Was the irrational/narcissistic alliance a prerequisite to the establishment of this joint new vocabulary? Probably. Instantly, Arnie Davis enjoined Dr. Potter. Potter became one of the Davis cats. What does this mean? Often, the clinician doesn't grasp a deeper understanding of the ways in which he serves as a selfobject for the patient until later in the treatment. Sometimes, the gap that is instantly filled may not be known until much later. Much happens as the therapeutic alliance matures. Not only is there often a key such as the Davis cat, but there is a process of entrance. Benedetti, the Swiss analyst from Italy, has described the therapeutic phenomenon where the patient, in psychosis, draws the doctor into a needed position within his internal psychic world. Here Potter is taken into the world of computers. He needs to draw on whatever his own experience is to allow mutuality to develop. He must be open to being touched by the patient in an emotional way. Sometimes, this means having feelings elicited that are unusual. The countertransference serves as information about the patient's emotional state. Sometimes, the emotions are dramatized in the countertransference in the clinician's thought, fantasy, or dream forms. We are reminded by

Racker (1968) that we should not ignore them. In contrast to Dr. Potter's work with Amy Mills, an intense set of countertransference phenomena did not mark the acknowledging phase of treatment with Arnie Davis but rather, the bearing and putting into perspective phases.

Back to the beginning. A joint system evolved. Within the computer talk, the files of the Beast and the agony of the Martyr were opened. With a focus on affect, myriad difficult experiences can be organized and clustered together. This is what Jung meant by the feeling-toned complex. By defining, delimiting, and labeling psychotic experience in terms of affect, the therapist and patient move through Semrad's first stage of therapy: acknowledging.

"THE DEN OF THE BEAST": AN ANSWERING MACHINE

Yet, how are Dr. Potter and Arnie Davis able to bear the Beast of anger and the Martyr of guilt? The simple answer is that these disturbing emotions are borne first by the therapeutic alliance and then within the patient.

As Dr. Potter's work with Arnie Davis continued into their second year, the patient obtained an answering machine. There were fewer messages left with secretaries when appointments needed to be changed, and there was more direct telephone contact. When attempting to reach the patient, Dr. Potter got Mr. Davis's machine, which said: "You have reached the den of the Beast. At the sound of the tone, please leave a message." Interestingly, during the past several months, Arnie Davis had stopped typing conversations with the Beast into computer files and he had stopped having the perceptual experiences of feeling himself to have fangs or certain tastes associated with the Beast. Yet, the Beast lived on in a different form. One form became tied to the work that the doctor and the patient were doing together. The Beast had now become integrated into the computer "tech" vocabulary that characterized the text of the therapeutic alliance. In this way, anger is borne by the shared language—it is, in this way, detoxified. We are reminded of Benedetti's (1987) notion of "progressive psychopathology"; as the patient recovers from psychosis, the form and content of the feeling-toned complex becomes less severe, less dissociated from the rest of the psyche—though the symptom remains, there is a "positivization" of it.

Was there an unconscious fusion, an "intersubjectivity" that lay below the common dialogue of the alliance? Stolorow, Brandchaft, and Atwood (1987) commented:

Essential to the structuralization of a sense of self is the acquisition of a firm belief in the validity of one's own subjective experiences. The early foundations of this belief are consolidated through the validating attunement of the caregiving surround to the child's perceptions and emotional reactions. When such early validating responsiveness has been consistently absent or grossly unreliable, the child's belief in his own subjective reality will remain unsteady and vulnerable to dissolution—a specific structural weakness that we regularly find as predisposing to psychotic states in later life. . . . Consistent empathic decoding of the patient's subjective truth gradually establishes the therapeutic bond as an archaic intersubjective context in which his belief in his own personal reality can become more firmly consolidated. (pp. 133–135)

The phrase "therapeutic symbiosis," coined by Harold Searles (1979) speaks to a dedifferentiation or fusion between doctor and patient. It is cast in terms of providing a place where the various fragments of a psychotic patient's experience can congeal. The therapist allows the matrix of his or her own psyche to be drawn into the fragmented parts of the patient. In this framework, a period of time must follow before the patient can differentiate out into a more coherent state of mental health.

Potter's work with Arnie Davis was slightly different from both these theoretical notions. Mr. Davis was already on the road to recovery when he recruited Dr. Potter. The underlying network of their alliance was not, palpably, archaic, yet the intersubjective characteristics of it were, nonetheless, quite present.

A SOMATIC UNION

The Boston psychiatrist, David Mann (1986), has worked and written extensively about psychosis and contends that psychotic patients have an "impulse to identify." The literature on identification and internalization in psychoanalysis and psychotherapy is lengthy (Meissner, 1976; Schafer, 1968) and the notions are embedded in a variety of theories. The odd somatic identifications of Arnie Davis may reflect an impulse to identify, yet there may be more. What do these identifications do? Does it make sense to speak of an identification with a selfobject?

The process of establishing a network of selfobject relationships that permit the patient to bear and integrate difficult affects is a part of self psychology put forward by the well-known Chicago psychoanalyst, Ernest Wolf. In his *Treating the Self* (1989), Wolf points to this process of recruiting new selfobjects in the patient's environment as being a signal of the patient's recovery. Wolf also points out different kinds of selfobject relationship needs that commonly occur over the life course, such as mirroring, idealizing, alter ego, adversarial, merger, and efficacy. The body part selfobject may be an additional form or variety of the alter ego need in this regard and may occur more frequently in work with patients who are or have been psychotic. Yet, in a way, these kinds of merger can be viewed as the initial ways in which the therapist is enlisted in the process of acknowledging, bearing, and putting into perspective unbearable affect.

Stolorow and Stolorow (1987) have asserted:

> Selfobject functions pertain fundamentally to the integration of affect into the organization of self-experience and that the need for selfobject ties pertains most centrally to the need for attuned responsiveness to affect states in all stages of the life cycle. (p. 66)

In the later states of recovery, as the fabric of the patient's psyche becomes capable of absorbing, holding, and "circulating" these affects, the enlistment process extends beyond the therapeutic dyad.

REMEMBERING, REPEATING, AND WORKING THROUGH

Freud's (1914) formula for psychoanalysis, "remember, repeat and work through," has its parallel in Semrad's "acknowledging, bearing, and putting into perspective" unbearable affect. Common elements characterize the working-through and the putting-into-perspective stages. Psychosynthesis rather than psychoanalysis is the primary thrust. The same themes, triggers, affects, and defensive maneuvers all recur but they do so with less frequency and with less intensity. New strategies have taken hold. Although the patient is still vulnerable to flare-ups, less disintegration occurs because unbearable affect is now able to be metabolized. The patient knows where it is coming from, historically, and is more aware of his or her own response. New networks can begin to take hold as well. Self-esteem is supported, and intolerable feelings have a safe place to be heard.

Is it required that Dr. Potter no longer be Tony the Tiger for the termination to occur? Does the clinician ever "terminate" with a psychotic patient? The modern rediscoverer of the primary process, Merton Gill, in his *Analysis of the Transference* (1982), stated that progression through treatment involved overcoming two kinds of resistances. The first was the resistance to the awareness of the transference. The second was the resistance to the resolution of the transference. If a selfobject environment is absolutely necessary to the ability to bear the unbearable, how could a clinician ever help a patient overcome Gill's second type of resistance? As treatment winds down, what happens?

MEN WHO GET RELIGION

For four years, Melanie, a 48-year-old woman with a 28-year history of bipolar affective disorder with mood-congruent psychotic features, had been in intensive psychotherapeutic treatment. She had done well with her pharmacotherapy of lithium, amitriptyline, and diazepam, which she had been on for almost 10 years. At the beginning of her psychotherapeutic work, she had also been taking Thioridazine, which was discontinued. At that time, she was profoundly depressed and vegetative, but she was not psychotic. The therapist only became acquainted with her psychosis when Melanie had a manic episode, about one year ago.

At that time, Melanie was visiting her son in California. She had also, recently, suffered from a bout of sciatic pain due to a herniated lumbar disc. Her son had just moved to Palo Alto to go to medical school. Her other son was finishing his sophomore year of college in a different state. This was the first time that both her boys were living in a different city than Boston, where she lived. During her manic psychosis, Melanie believed that she was independently wealthy and that she should be a senator or, perhaps, a religious leader—a rabbi. However, when she mentioned these ideas in therapy, she quickly "took them back" since "religion wasn't something to kid about." Her lithium was adjusted upward by a local California psychiatrist and she came back home to Boston.

The therapist and the patient discussed what had happened. Melanie's focus, in the treatment, had been on her relationship with her mother who was now 74 years old. Melanie related that her mother was still a very indifferent and demanding, selfish woman. The therapist began to ask more about the loss of the men in her life and the patient began to talk about her late husband. Her husband, Edward, died suddenly, in a car accident. The oldest son, Bobby, had to become the "man of the family" at the age of 12. Melanie remarked that she had depended on both her boys and her brother for emotional support after her husband's death. It was discovered that she had depended a great deal on Ed during the marriage and tended to see him as a strong reliable figure.

The therapist wondered whether his being male played a role in the transference. He felt that it did. Melanie had adored her father, who was an orthodox Jewish scholar. Despite her mother's indifference, Melanie had felt unconditionally loved by her attentive dad. He had died shortly after her marriage to Ed. Although her boys were raised Jewish and had Bar Mitzvahs, Ed had no interest in Judaism, even though he was raised Jewish. Melanie stopped going to synagogue on a regular basis because Ed wasn't willing to participate.

Over time, Melanie revealed that the perfect picture of her husband, Ed, was not so perfect. Although he was decisive, he didn't seem to have been very tuned into her. In fact, he was quite inattentive at times. She revealed that their sex life had not been gratifying to her at all. While Melanie talked about the therapist's importance to her and as she discussed the role of men in her life, she had a serious exacerbation of her sciatica and lumbar disc problem. She was hospitalized for three months and it was unclear whether she would be able to return to work. At the time, she seemed emotionally desperate, but she did not decompensate. She needed to have many sessions over the phone. Interestingly, she decided on her own to contact her old rabbi and she reconnected with her old synagogue—the one she had belonged to at the beginning of her marriage.

You could see that important old values were returning in new forms. Melanie started dating again. Six years ago, she had met a man with whom she fell in love. But, as she pushed for a commitment from him then, he pulled away. He had been married before and Melanie felt that he had never gotten over his first wife. Melanie dated other people but this prior boyfriend remained special to her because "they could laugh, they liked each other." When he called again during a crisis with one of his children, they began dating again. This time she was less deferential and she decided that she didn't really need a marriage commitment. He, in fact, responded well to her new strength. The therapist was interested but not totally surprised to hear that this man, Manny, was an orthodox Jew. She had mentioned this before. Melanie and Manny began to date and she commented that their sex life together was excellent despite "our middle age."

In a parallel fashion, Melanie became more comfortable with her anger. Before, it had been unbearable and she dealt with it by turning it against herself—her self-esteem would plummet. She would also, from time to time, get "hyper" or "manic" and compensate by taking on ideas that she was a nationally important and powerful figure—a senator. As her unbearable affects became tolerable in the context of her psychotherapy and as she learned about the role that men had played in her life and her need for their attention to offset her mother's indifference, she began to change. Melanie commented that she felt more able to tell her sons that they were being inconsiderate or demanding when they would want to bring friends home from school on short notice or when they needed money in a hurry. She received enthusiastic support for her new expression of her anger from her therapist, Manny, and the rabbi.

Melanie also began to see herself in a slightly different light. She felt that she did have a lot to offer. She began to feel that her perseverance in the light of her bipolar illness, the loss of her husband, her frightening back injury, and her coping with financial stress spoke to her being a woman of integrity and character. The therapist had felt this way about her all along, and now she was able to say it about herself. As she experienced herself as being "believed in" (Havens, 1994) and as she came to understand the circumstances through which she had lost faith in herself, Melanie began to believe in herself. Melanie was now independently wealthy **in character** and was able to fully represent herself. This was the transformation of her grandiosity; here was the healthy evolution of her rich lady senator delusions into legitimate pride.

In the course of her treatment, Melanie was able to put her intolerable affects into perspective, they no longer dominated her psychic life. The recovery process demonstrated her new ability to "enlist" an affectively responsive network of idealizing selfobjects. The therapist, the rabbi, and her boyfriends, like her father before, could help her bear the unbearable affects generated by the indifference of her mother and husband.

In summary, unbearable affect is borne by the therapeutic relationship and by the reestablishment of missing self-regard. As Freud (1914) advised, the process of remembering, repeating in the transferences of the here and now, and working through psychic conflict and distress allows for the unconscious to become conscious in a therapeutic way. With a focus on affect in psychosis, Semrad's (Khantzian et al., 1969) modification of this process involves the detoxification of unbearable affect through a discussion of its origins. Added onto this notion is the necessary dimension of what the therapist provides for the patient. Not only is therapy a forum for discussion but it is a means through which essential psychic functions may be reestablished. This is what "psychosynthesis" refers to in the psychotherapy of psychosis. Arnie Davis is able to refind someone who will help him with his inner Beast; Melanie finds someone who will help her with her sadness and anger at being neglected. These therapists are experienced in specific ways, the patients use them to fill in missing parts of the self; they fill the narcissistic gap. As unbearable affects gets further put into perspective, new members of the crew are taken on board. The patient, once shipwrecked and alienated by psychosis, now knows that he or she does not have to go it alone. Others can continue to contribute in essential ways. Should storm clouds arise, how much easier it is to deal with what may come into one's path.

11

STAYING OUT
OF PSYCHOSIS

It is equally fatal for the mind to have a system and to have none. It will simply have to decide to combine the two.

—Von Schlegel

BEYOND PSYCHOSIS: ARNIE DAVIS

Just three days ago, Tony had received the letter from Amy Mills. Now he was having some trouble concentrating on what Arnie Davis was saying . . . something about his new cat fighting with the old ones . . . .

Arnie: You look like you're tired. I'll see you next week.

Tony: (returning to the session) No, actually I'm not tired.

Arnie: (smiling) Maybe you need to stop staying up so late.

Tony: (recognizing that Arnie was teasing him and that Arnie could now feel the refocus of Tony's attention) You figure you have an impaired physician on your hands?

Arnie: Nah, you're OK . . . I think.

Tony: I'm a good cat?

(Here Tony mixes together past events, current events, and the transference—he knows that Arnie's father was a Beast, that he was taken in as Tony the Tiger, and that Arnie was frustrated now, as his old cats were fighting with the new one he had recently brought home.)

Arnie: A lot better than Sparkle. That animal is going to drive me crazy. All night, I hear hissing and screeching. I know they'll get to know each other and everything will be all right . . . but, geeez. . . . rubbing his wrist . . .

Tony: Is your wrist OK?

Arnie: I scratched it when I threw the glass at the wall . . . it's no big deal (sees the surprised look on Tony's face) . . . nobody got hurt, Ethyl wasn't even home . . . the cats were in the other room . . . (Arnie is lost in thought)

I told you about the old landlord threatening to sue us? That prick claims we still owe him $150. It's ridiculous. I left that place spotless and we never got our security deposit back. Now he says he may sue us because he had to have a cleaning service come in. . . . Let him just try.

Tony: What? Not this landlord?

Arnie: It's not this landlord, it's the last one. The sonofabitch says we owe him $150 . . . it'll be a cold day in hell before he sees that money . . . I'll make him pay for lawyers, court costs, serving a subpoena . . . If I knew how, I'd really like to get him . . . (with a look of delight)

Tony: (on cue) How?

Arnie: I'd get into his bank account with my computer and modem and erase his balance. I'd love to see the look on his face when his bank bounced his check and he says, "Uh, wait a minute . . . where's all my money? . . ."

Somehow in the midst of the dialogue, Tony's mind was stuck on the image of Arnie's glass splintering as it hit the wall. He knew that Arnie was doing well. Yes, he was still vulnerable to feeling assaulted and guilty, but the anger was more tempered . . . the cut was from cleaning up the glass and was an accident—not intentional—the anger/motor episodes were infrequent; only three over the past year, and no doubt, some sleep deprivation from Arnie's new "child" made things worse. The feeling-toned complex of Beast-father-kitten-child was now much more tied into the usual fabric of Arnie's day-to-day life. Rarely did it overwhelm him.

Yet, there was something about the smashed-glass image that wouldn't leave Tony's mind. His mind wandered back to Amy Mills. He had received a letter from her saying that she had just been admitted to a psychiatric unit in Manhattan. She wrote that she had been dating a guy who hung around the theater where she worked. It turned out that her roommate had also liked this guy. The roommate felt that Amy had "stolen" him from her and wouldn't hear Amy's protests otherwise. Amy offered to stop seeing him, but her roommate left. Amy didn't have enough money to stay in the apartment for more than a month. The voices had started to come back. She had started walking around the streets of Manhattan and was picked up by the police who brought her to the hospital. Who was she looking for?

What had really distracted the therapist even more during his session with Arnie was Tony's image of himself smashing a glass. Six months ago, Tony and Nancy had been married in a nice outdoor ceremony near Harvard yard. Neither Tony nor Nancy was very religious; she was half-Jewish and half-Lutheran and both of his parents were Jewish. A reform rabbi had performed the service.

Toward the end of the session with Arnie, Tony started to realize what the smashing glass was all about. It had to do with the end of the marriage ceremony. It didn't take much of what Arnie was now saying to bring him back, full force, into the session.

Arnie: What do you think about guns?

Tony: They are usually instruments of death, no?

Arnie: Maybe they are good for protection. After all, Ethyl and I don't live in the greatest neighborhood.

(After Robert Meyer's suicide, Tony had no tolerance for his patients owning guns.)

Tony: I don't want you to have a gun around. I'm sorry, but they are just not safe. Statistically, there's a 10,000 time greater chance that you or Ethyl will be killed by that gun than any intruder.

Arnie: Well . . . it makes me feel safer . . . I've had one for years . . .

Tony: You never mentioned it . . .

Arnie: I never use it. Maybe on New Year's Eve, I'll fire off some blanks at midnight . . .

Tony: So, you have no bullets . . .

Arnie: No, I do have bullets . . .

Tony: Are they in the gun?

Arnie: No, but I keep the gun and bullets in the drawer in my nightstand . . . I don't have children so nobody can get at it . . . I mean, the cats can't load the thing (smiles and gestures).

Tony: (not amused) Still, there are zillions of home gun accidents each year . . .

Arnie: (interrupts) Ethyl hates guns so she doesn't come near it . . .

Tony: (interrupts) So, why have it at all? (pressing) (long pause)

Arnie: You know, when I sat down at the computer to write that SOB old landlord a nasty letter back in his face, I had the gun right by the computer . . .

Tony: Great, so you could shoot yourself in the head? Or, perhaps, shoot the computer? (genuinely upset; perhaps slightly paternal; deliberately facetious)

Arnie: No, it wasn't me that I was angry with . . . I'm not interested in hurting myself . . . and I'm not interested in hurting somebody else . . . I mean, I'm not about to go and shoot some stupid asshole landlord and spend my life in jail . . . I mean I may be crazy but I'm not stupid . . . (waits to see if Tony chuckles, sees that Tony is not laughing) . . . it just gave me a sense of having some power.

Tony: Perhaps the two of us can think of some other ways of dealing with your feelings of powerlessness.

After Tony negotiated for Arnie to get rid of the gun, he wondered if he had done the right thing or the wrong thing. Here Arnie wasn't "turning against himself," yet was his "identification with the aggressor" any more healthy? Arnie seemed upbeat as he left and agreed to dispose of the weapon. Tony remembered an old supervisor of his from Mount Sinai telling him that it was important to take the patient's weapons away, whatever they were—objects, not showing up for sessions, not paying the fee . . . .

Again, the image of the shattering glass came back as he sat alone after the session. The rabbi had said that the breaking of the glass at the end of wedding ceremony symbolized the "destruction of the temple"—Tony hadn't a clue as to what temple they were talking about. Someone else had said that it was to scare evil spirits away. But the rabbi also mentioned that the breaking of the glass symbolized the fragility of marriage. It takes a long time to build a strong relationship, yet it is vulnerable to being broken in an instant.

Here's where Amy's note fit in. You work so hard together to make what is unbearable bearable. Then, something happens and psychosis steps up to take you back in. Has there been any healing?

That night, Tony dreamed that he was running through the streets of Manhattan trying to find Donald Jones. To tell him to let go of Amy Mills, that he, Dr. Potter would take her back to Boston where she would be OK. In the dream, he was running down one street and then another, in the dark. He couldn't find Donald Jones. He felt a sense of desperation and then, loss, in the dream.

When he awoke, Tony realized that the shattering glass image had been amplified by his original introduction to psychosis. His New York running partner, Andrew Stevens, from Tony's medical school days, had smashed the painted mirror in his father's apartment building. What had become of Andrew?

Since the start of his residency, Tony had worked with about 30 psychotic patients in intensive psychotherapy. Most had made good progress, some had not. Robert Meyer's suicide was far from success with psychosis. Jack Barnes was still in the halfway house connected with Mount Sinai. Jack had not been in contact with Tony, nor vise versa since Tony had left. Word had it that Jack was working with another resident. This time it was a woman. Tony had heard that Jack had gotten a maintenance job. So, something was happening. Had his work with Jack made a difference? Tony remembered the Hippocratic Oath: "Above all, do no harm." Psychotherapy could definitely have negative side effects, but he didn't think he had harmed Jack Barnes. Wouldn't it be easier just to treat psychosis with somatic therapy? One could then just focus one's worry more on the drug and less on the patient. He struggled to keep in mind that progress was a "three steps forward, two steps backward" kind of affair.

Tony also resolved to call Amy Mills the next day. Was calling his old patient in Manhattan a way of avoiding thinking of himself as a failure? No, Tony felt he could live with failure. Rather, he wanted to attenuate any feelings that Amy might have that her rehospitalization was a failure on her part. Where's a woman to stay in Manhattan when her roommate runs out on her and she has no money? Some kind of asylum is warranted, no? It was not that he believed that the treatment would start anew over the phone, but perhaps, he could be of some help to Amy as she attempted to regain her footing. He believed in her and he knew that, at times of setback, self-doubt can run rampant. Staying out of psychosis means that if you get back in, you get back out as soon as possible. You need to believe in yourself.   ✦

THE CURE OR CARE OF PSYCHOSIS

No doubt, Dr. Potter struggles with the same questions as do hundreds of other clinicians. Do psychotic patients truly heal? Or, is the treatment palliative; the wound bandaged over, only to flare up again with a new external irritant? Is there lasting change? And, if so, what kind? How does it occur? Many experts will argue that lasting change is quite achievable with psychotherapy with psychotic patients (Benedetti, 1987; Havens, 1986; Karon & VandenBos, 1981; Rosen, 1968; Searles, 1965). Others would suggest that treatment is palliative and that it doesn't matter whether insight or support is provided (Gunderson et al., 1984). Still, other professionals will assert that psychotic patients can stay reasonably healthy but they require a lifelong therapist or counselor (Benedetti, 1987).

For most asthmatics or diabetics, the length of time leading into an episode and the length of time in the episode impact significantly on what the physician can expect in terms of the amount of time needed to get the patient out of the episode and the amount of time necessary for rehabilitation back to health. The same is true for mental illness. The natural history of psychosis and its impact on the individual is quite variable. This kind of a view already holds sway. The clinician naturally assumes that the patient who is chronic is not likely to get well. Here, the forces of illness and morbidity have held power for so long that any natural healing tendencies of the individual have long been overwhelmed. Does it make sense to ally with the few remaining healthy fragments of the patient to take on such odds?

Who can know for sure? Dr. Potter's patient Jack Barnes may be successful with his new woman resident in ways that were not possible with a male psychiatrist. So much remains unknown about the potential keys to success in the psychological treatment of psychosis. It's no wonder that so much attention has been directed toward somatic treatments. One can delimit the field of inquiry to a great degree. The psychological and interpersonal variables in the psychological treatment of psychosis seem unending. Should Potter consider the Mills rehospitalization to be a failure? Should he view it as merely a relapse? Time will tell.

The mistake here is in the concept of cure. Few medical illnesses are cured. After an infectious illness is treated with an antibiotic and the infection has cleared, it is considered a cure. Interestingly, in Breuer and Freud's early work (Breuer & Freud, 1893/1981), unbearable affect was to the pathogenic idea in the mind as fever was to the infectious germ. Is a potential recurrence of illness more likely in the same part of the individual? Is there a mix between host and environment that makes reinfection or a new outbreak more likely? Carefully consider the analogy. A child gets a sore throat from another student at school. A penicillin derivative "cures" it. With repeated sore throats, one looks both at the school as well as the tonsils. Perhaps the doctor takes a look at the immune system, especially if the child stays sick when he or she is no longer in an infectious environment.

Those who work with psychosis do the same. Not only the brain is examined but the patient's psyche as well. How will the forces of health be marshaled? One may first return to Havens's (1986) concept of performative statements. The physician must attempt to identify what is healthy about the patient. What capacities are already present that can bear the unbearable? Our attention is directed toward self-esteem. In Kraepelin's tripartite mind, we return to the will. Thus, facilitating a strong will, renewing hope, and assisting the patient in making choices may all go a long way toward helping the patient weather potentially stormy situations.

With patients saying bad things to themselves, initially through the vehicle of voices and later through loud thoughts, the clinician may attempt to strengthen Kraepelin's second part of the mind—cognition. What are the thoughts that lead to speech? Helping the patient stop self-criticism (Garfield, 1985) can provide real resilience toward holding and circulating difficult affects.

The glue that holds the psyche together is emotion. Recall Bleuler's (Bleuler, 1905/1950) assertion: "Affectivity is the basis of life." With an ability to both freely express and, at the same time, hold emotions in check, a patient, now "out" of psychosis, is best able to steer clear of dangerous weather. As Potter's work with Arnie Davis demonstrates, even when the patient is out of psychosis, the feeling-toned complex remains. Charles Brenner (1982), New York's modern-day Freud, has written extensively about mental conflict from the classical psychoanalytic perspective. He remarks that conflict does not disappear, even in neurosis. Once again, the concept of cure is misleading. What we are looking for is a strengthening of the psyche, the clinician seeks an "enabling." The self becomes more coherent, more cohesive, more positively colored with emotion. In good care, the pathology is detoxified as the healthy tissue is fortified. Conflict and deficit are always addressed. In good care, the patient is able to navigate the vicissitudes of his or her life less threatened by the stormy effects of psychic conflict. As conflict softens and deficit strengthens, affects are flowing in a more integrated and free fashion. What sort of change become visible in the patient as this happens?

THEORIES OF CHANGE IN THE PSYCHOTHERAPY OF PSYCHOSIS

Arlow and Brenner (1969) take the classical view that psychosis represents extremes of defense operating within the frame of normal psychic conflict. They posit no "deficit" condition in the psychology of psychosis. Health is regained through a psychoanalytic treatment where psychic conflict is analyzed and where, eventually, the unconscious is made conscious (Bion, 1960; Klein, 1930; Rosenfeld, 1965). The hallmark of success would be seen in a maturation of the kinds of defenses that the patient utilizes. Defensive operations would move from projection, denial, and distortion to rationalization, hypochondriasis, and repression. Psychotic defenses would be replaced by more neurotic ones.

In the object relations school (Meissner, 1978; Modell, 1968; Rosen, 1968; Searles, 1979; Winnicott, 1965) a holding environment is created wherein split, pathogenic internal images of self and others are allowed to come together under the auspices of transference experience. The recreation of a safe therapeutic symbiosis allows for the butterfly to come out of the cocoon. Psychotic ambivalence transforms into neurotic mixed feelings. The clinician may become a positive internalized figure. In a model similar to that proposed by Mahler (1972) for the subphases of separation and individuation, the psychotic patient develops the capacity for object constancy. "Now that I can carry you with me inside myself, I can go it alone." A termination can occur because the doctor is carried around as a positive internal resource within the patient.

The American psychoanalyst, Harry Stack Sullivan (1954), laid the groundwork for how social or interpersonal psychiatric interventions can heal psychosis. Sullivan believed that psychosis was active only within the context of a given clinical/social situation. The patient, who is often, too much into him- or herself, constantly labors under the weight of what others presumably think about him or her. The trick, then, is to be aware of how the patient feels about what others think. "Part of the interviewer's development of skill comes from observing, more or less automatically, what is 'probably' the case with respect to the interviewee's feeling about the interviewer's attitude." (p. 192) Sullivan's emphasis was on not humiliating the patient, while, at the same time, fully understanding the emotional state of the patient. This is a similar approach to psychosis as the one advocated here where, in the context of self-esteem preservation, a focus on emotion is at the heart of the treatment.

A NEW VIEW ON THE CARE OF PSYCHOSIS

As psychotic patients master the emotions that are so tumultuous for them; as unbearable affect is acknowledged, borne, and put into perspective, specific changes take place. The "positivization of symptoms" that Benedetti (1987) alluded to are representative of internal changes. Does the fragmented self reaneal? Again, the Chicago analyst, Ernest Wolf (1993), provides some clues. From the standpoint of self psychology, Wolf believes that a specific process in psychotherapy is responsible for building strength into the patient. This is what he calls the cycle of empathic disruption and repair. Within an ongoing selfobject transference, the patient encounters rifts in the attunement of doctor to the patient. The copilot fails to do a task and puts the boat at risk. The patient, who has temporarily lost the use of the right hand, then falls apart, to a greater or lesser extent and reexperiences an acute need.

Next, the copilot catches his or her own mistake and rights the error. The crew becomes whole once again. The clinician becomes reattuned and learns much from these mistakes. More importantly, the patient experiences relief; there is fulfillment of the renewed need and internal cohesiveness is reestablished. Emotions are stirred up and the threat of psychosis returns. Yet, with repair of empathic rupture, emotions are permitted to settle down into new patterns. The psychic glue of emotion forms new bonds for the reconfiguration and reassembly of an internally fragmented self. In this way, the patient is permitted a kind of self-confidence that comes from having fears generated and then alleviated. In a very basic sense, there is an increased ability to tolerate frustration in the belief that things can get better. Does this process occur in patients who are susceptible to psychosis?

Amy Mills sees Tony Potter with his fiancee, Nancy, in a restaurant, and the patient is in turmoil. Hard work and attention to the pain mends the alliance (a selfobject transference restoration). Arnie Davis sees that his doctor is not paying attention to him and once again, experiences himself as unworthy. Is it his fault? Is he guilty again? The self becomes unsettled. The boat begins to sway. Yet, the doctor comes back and through words or deeds acknowledges the disruption such that things now come back into alignment. As intolerable emotions are, within the confines of a safe place, inevitably reignited and then defused, new roots of affectivity can be laid. When the indicators of health become evident, such as when a patient enlists others in the process of acknowledging, bearing, and putting into perspective difficult emotions, then successful care can be said to have been administered.

Wolf's theory of self-renewal echoes the great existentialists of the past. Perhaps, most notably, is the work of Binswanger (1945) with his psychotic patient "Ilse." In that case, Ilse was psychologically trapped by a tyrannical, abusive father and an ineffective mother. At the age of 39, after watching a theater performance of *Hamlet*, Ilse, now married with three children herself, decided that she must convince her father, through some dramatic act, to treat her mother with more compassion. Ilse felt that Hamlet had missed his chance to save himself from insanity by not sanctifying his father's memory by killing the King at prayer. Ilse set up her plan for her own father. One day, after having been scolded again by him, Ilse told him that she knew a way to save him and she stuck her right arm into her parent's burning stove. She then took it out and held her hand toward him saying "Look, this is to show you how much I love you!" Ilse's energetic, self-mutilating grandiosity was somewhat tempered when her father, shocked by her act, briefly changed his attitude, but when he relapsed to cruel behavior toward her mother and when Ilse, herself, lost a child, she became increasingly grandiose and self-referential; she became convinced that everyone was sneering at her. Binswanger's treatment consisted of establishing a direct, feeling, relationship to the patient and an active engagement of the split-off father theme. Whereas the classical school drew out conflict from within the patient and sought to analyze it away, the object relations school attempted to hold it. Whereas the interpersonal school attempted to undercut the roots of conflict, the existential approach was to leap into it. Binswanger established an ongoing contact with Ilse's experience. Here was the method of empathic attunement. Oscillations of emotion between therapist and patient were at its core.

How close the self psychologists are to the methods of existential psychoanalysis! Note that Wolf's methods expand on Binswanger's. If Binswanger asserted that psychosis lay in the obstacles to understanding, then Wolf points out that the recurrence of such obstacles in the process of treatment is inevitable, and in fact, the continual clearing away of them is the process by which sickness is dispelled. Thus, within the therapeutic relationship, affective disruption and restoration afford the patient the requisite experiences to stay out of psychosis.

Thus, the affect approach to psychosis cuts across all the main schools of psychoanalysis in theory. It draws from the classical school in its feeling-toned complex, the interpersonal school in its attention to the affective response to threats to self-esteem, the object relations school in how emotion transforms itself and the existential and self psychology schools in its emphasis on empathic emotional attunement. At the same time, by keeping the North Star of affect always in sight, the practicing clinician never gets lost in the sea of theory.

The mobilization, active circulation, and tempering of emotion that characterizes being out of psychosis is a life's work. In working with psychotic patients, no doubt Dr. Potter, along with the existential and self psychology psychoanalysts, would agree. As emotion shifts from perception, through the body and into cognition, the doctor and the patient find their way out together. At some point, the treatment comes to a close. Either it is artificially interrupted because of a move, a change of employment, or death, or sometimes, there is a mutual decision to wind things down—the frequency decreases; perhaps there is even some kind of a formal "termination." Yet, almost always the door remains open.

The most important door to remain open is that of the previously psychotic patient to his or her own affects. This is where the process of enlistment comes into play; a strong therapeutic impulse, kindled by the treatment, is carried on by the patient such that emotion can be actively experienced, circulated, and metabolized. Yet, what can be said about the role of the clinician in the posttreatment time? Should there be no contact?

POSTTREATMENT AFFECTIVE ACCESS

As Benedetti and Furlan (1987) state in their review of 29 completed psychotherapies with psychotic patients:

> These cases show that there is a correlation between the deep affection of the therapeutic relationship, clinical improvement, and maintenance of posttherapeutic contact. Certainly someone might criticize such behavior as an unresolved therapeutic relationship; perhaps that judgment would be true in cases of neurosis. (p. 202)

It makes sense that the psychiatrist, having been an important person in the patient's life, would continue to have some place in the future emotional life of the patient. If nothing more, the door would be left open to the positive memories of emotional connection and stability regained. Thus, at a minimum, the therapist is put into perspective as a positive way station as the patient continues on in his or her own life. More often, what one finds, is that staying out of psychosis means staying in touch with the clinician in some way or another.

This need is particularly true when the treatment has been artificially interrupted before it can run its natural course. In those cases, the therapist can serve as an emotional liaison to the new clinician or enlistees. And, with patients who have completed treatment, an open door is more than symbolic. As Amy Mills runs into trouble, her instinct is to write to Dr. Potter. Again, her letter, in the postherapeutic period is a form of enlistment. His response is crucial. Renewed emotional contact is essential for Amy to continue to make her way and, as best as she can, to stay out of psychosis.

The demands of working with psychotic patients are enormous. The profession requires that the adage for becoming a gifted writer also be true for the doctor. The gifted writer, it was said, always feels that "nothing human disgusts me." Although true for the psychotherapist of psychotic patients, a corollary statement must also be true; that "everything human intrigues me." To embrace emotion as being at the heart of psychosis makes it possible to pursue the extraordinary and bring it into the world of the day to day. To be successful at helping patients stay out of psychosis, the clinician must, in addition, find that which is extraordinary within the vacant lot of those wrecked by psychosis and enlist it in the cause of healing.

BITTERSWEET SEPARATION

In the 6th year of treatment, Sally has begun to see her therapist less frequently. She has had no paranoid episodes for over a year. She comes in about once or twice a month. Her job is going well, her relationship with her family is on a new footing. She no longer plays the role as the baby of the family. There has been a rearrangement in those relationships. Her family is still supportive of her in general, but she navigates her way with them such that she receives little critique and little adoration. All in all, this makes her feel more mature; she has remarked on several occasions that she respects herself more now.

She still sees Bob. She loves him a lot but the religious issue is a big one for her. He is Catholic; she is Jewish. Also, he feels that he is not ready for children and although she is uncertain herself about how she would do as a mother, she thinks she will want to give it a try. She knows that she will be more attentive than her own mother was, but now she also admires her mother in other ways. What the clinician noticed most about her at this time is the bittersweet quality of her mood. She is somewhat sad, but strong. She is conflicted about the present but optimistic about the future. If she breaks it off with Bob, even temporarily, would he go back with her if she decides that he is the one? Maybe he would come around with regard to kids and religion if she could hold her ground. The therapist can't give Sally answers but can fully appreciate her dilemma. Not infrequently, in the psychotherapy of psychosis, the natural disaster of psychotic storms is transformed into the simple conundrum of not knowing exactly where one wants to go.

The therapist begins to realize that Sally is in the termination phase of her work in therapy. In Sally's case, one is reminded of Melanie Klein's (1946) shift from the paranoid-schizoid position to the depressed position. Sally is not clinically depressed, but she does experience the loss associated with giving up psychosis. Reality is distasteful.

There have been many understandings and misunderstandings between Sally and her therapist. Sally asked him about being a father and quickly commented, "Of course, you don't like to talk about yourself." The topic of making contact with the emotional life of the therapist was discussed in light of the unavailability of her mom when she was young. Sally confessed that for a long time, it hurt her that the therapist didn't share any of his inner emotional life with her. She acknowledged that the clinician did change his approach and that she has experienced him as having been more accessible. She smiled at times during this phase of the treatment. It was a melancholy sort of smile, and it made the therapist feel a little sad. Sally had developed her own eyes—she sees things pretty clearly. She had her own two feet solidly under her now and, with her own two hands, she had been managing whatever choppy situations arose with good dexterity.

She is seriously considering a separation from her boyfriend Bob. Maybe she'll come back to him, maybe she'll go on. The therapist realized that she may be speaking about him as well. Sally would still want consultation on her independent situation, yet, with much more access to her own emotional life, with guilt and anger more easily tolerated, psychosis was not a current threat. The patient and therapist concluded that although her separation from Bob may be a heartbreaker, that both he and she would survive and go on. He'll be OK. She'll be OK. Alone or together. She comments that through all the breakups and coming back together, she has grown a tremendous amount in her relationship with him. The therapist asked if the same was true for the two of them. Sally wondered if the clinician had some distant plans to move away. He said, "No, just that it is important that you have the freedom to determine what you need for yourself, not only with Bob but with your therapy as well." Sally remarked that she thought she would need the therapist more than ever now that she was becoming more independent. She remarked that she wanted to come back again in a few weeks to talk over the separation from Bob.

In summary, staying out of psychosis requires not only psychoanalytic work but psychosynthetic work as well. Insofar as unbearable affect shatters the patient's inner rudder, both conflict and deficit must simultaneously be addressed. Conflict is most clearly seen in Jung's (1970/1976) feeling-toned complex. Its force can be seen to rearrange the natural elements of the mind according to affect's own composition. Additionally, the affective bonds that bind cognition and volition together are twisted out of shape by the internal turmoil. With a determined eye on affect, clinicians are afforded an opportunity to serve as a copilot to those who have been thrown asunder by the storms of psychosis. First, through affect diagnosis, the therapist sounds the depths, measures the intensity and velocity of the forces at work and, through careful observation, comes to know the type of storm that has thrown the patient's life off course.

Next, through affect therapeutics, the therapist must find and fill the specific emotional requirement that will allow the patient to regain control over his or her own ship. As the bond between doctor and patient develops, the requisite functions of an able-bodied crew emerge. No two patients are alike, and thus no two psychotic storms are ever the same. The patient in need requires essential emotional contact with the therapist. Only then can the individual ride out the storm. As the day-to-day work of staying alive at sea continues, affective resonance will inevitably ebb and flow. It is through these experiences of being lost and being refound, in an emotional way, that a patient can realign his or her internal state. Therein, resolve is strengthened.

Most often, insight will follow healing. Knowing now what it takes for them to stay on course, patients will readily seek out new crew members who are able to assist them with those unavoidable spells of bad weather. Conflict recedes and deficit is repaired. These actions occur simultaneously and mutually influence each other. By using affect to chart the course out of psychosis, clinicians enable patients to become better navigators of their own destiny.

REFERENCES

Alexander, F., & French, T. (1946). *Psychoanalytic therapy: Principles and applications*. New York: Ronald Press.

Andreasen, N. C., & Olsen, S. (1982). Negative vs. positive schizophrenia: Definition and validation. *Archives of General Psychiatry, 39,* 789–794.

Arieti, S. (1955). *Interpretation of schizophrenia*. New York: Basic Books.

Arlow, J., & Brenner, C. (1969). The psychopathology of the psychoses: A proposed revision. *International Journal of Psycho-Analysis, 50,* 5–14.

Benedetti, G. (1987). *Psychotherapy of schizophrenia*. New York: New York University Press.

Benedetti, G., & Furlan, P. (1987). Individual psychoanalytic psychotherapy of schizophrenia. In G. Benedetti (Ed.), *Psychotherapy of schizophrenia* (pp. 198–212). New York: New York University Press.

Beres, D., & Arlow, J. A. (1974). Fantasy and identification in empathy. *Psychoanalytic Quarterly, 43,* 26–50.

Binswanger, L. (1945). Insanity as life-historical phenomenon and as mental disease: The case of Ilse. In R. May (Ed.), *Existence*. New York: Touchstone.

Bion, W. (1960). Note on the theory of schizophrenia. In *Second thoughts*. London: Heinemann Press.

Bleuler, E. (1926). Affectivitat, suggestibilitat, paranoia (2nd ed.). Halle. Translation in *New York State Hospital Bulletin*, February 1912. (Original work published 1906)

Bleuler, E. (1950). *Dementia praecox or the group of schizophrenias*. New York: International Universities Press. (Original work published 1905)

Brenner, C. (1982). *The mind in conflict*. New York: International Universities Press.

Breuer, J., & Freud, S. (1981). On the psychical mechanism of hysterical phenomena: Preliminary communication. In J. Strachey (Ed.), *The complete psychological works of Sigmund Freud, standard edition (Vol. 1)*. London: Hogarth Press. (Original work published 1893)

Bruch, H. (1974). *Learning psychotherapy*. Cambridge, MA: Harvard University Press.

Burke, K. (1969). *A grammar of motives*. Berkeley, CA: University of California Press.

Ciompi, L. (1994). *The concept of affect logic*. Lecture at the XIth International Symposium for the Psychotherapy of Schizophrenia, Washington, DC, June 12, 1994.

Cleghorn, J., Franco, S., Saechtman, B., Kaplan, R., Saechtman, H., Brown, G., Nahmias, C., & Garnett, S. (1992). Toward a brain map of auditory hallucinations. *American Journal of Psychiatry, 149*(8), 1062–1069.

Colby, K. M. (1981). Modeling a paranoid mind. *Behavioral and Brain Sciences, 4*, 515–560.

Cummings, J. (1985). Organic delusions: Phenomenology, anatomical correlations, and review. *British Journal of Psychiatry, 146*, 184–197.

Ellenberger, H. (1970). *The discovery of the unconscious*. New York: Basic Books, p. 301.

Federn, P. (1953). *Ego psychology and the psychoses*. London: Maresfield Reprints.

Fliess, R. (1959). On the nature of human thought: The primary and the secondary processes as exemplified by the dream and other psychic productions. In M. Levitt (Ed.), *Readings in psychoanalytic psychology* (pp. 213–220). New York: Appleton-Century-Crofts.

Freedman, N., & Grand, S. (Eds.). (1976). *Communicative structures and psychic structures*. New York: Plenum Press.

Freeman, T. (1963). The concept of narcissism in schizophrenic states. *International Journal of Psycho-Analysis, 44*, 293–303.

Freud, S. (1895). Project for a scientific psychology. In J. Strachey (Ed.), *Standard edition* (Vol. 1, pp. 335–346). London: Hogarth Press.

Freud, S. (1900). The interpretation of dreams. In. J. Strachey (Ed.), *Standard edition* (Vols. 4 & 5). London: Hogarth Press.

Freud, S. (1901a). On dreams. In J. Strachey (Ed.), *Standard edition* (Vol. 5). London: Hogarth Press.

Freud, S. (1901b). The psychopathology of everyday life. In J. Strachey (Ed.), *Standard edition* (Vol. 6). London: Hogarth Press.

Freud, S. (1912). Papers on technique. The dynamics of transference. In J. Strachey (Ed.), *Standard edition* (Vol. 12, pp. 97–108). London: Hogarth Press.

Freud, S. (1914). On narcissism: An introduction. In J. Strachey et al. (Eds.), *Standard edition* (Vol. 14, pp. 67–102). London: Hogarth Press.

Freud, S. (1923). The ego and the id. In J. Strachey (Ed.), *Standard edition* (Vol. 14, pp. 1–16). London: Hogarth Press.

Freud, S. (1958). Project for a scientific psychology. In J. Strachey (Ed.), *Standard edition* (Vol. 3). London: Hogarth Press. (Original work published 1895)

Freud, S. (1958). Psychoanalytic notes on an autobiographical account of a case of paranoia (dementia paranoids). In J. Strachey et al. (Eds.), *Standard edition* (Vol. 12, pp. 1–82). London: Hogarth Press. (Original work published 1911)

Freud, S. (1958). Remembering, repeating and working through. In J. Strachey (Ed.), *Standard edition* (Vol. 12, pp. 145–156). London: Hogarth Press. (Original work published 1914)

Freud, S. (1961). The loss of reality in psychosis and neurosis. In J. Strachey (Ed.), *Standard edition* (Vol. 19, pp. 181–187). London: Hogarth Press. (Original work published 1924)

Freud. S. (1962). Further remarks on the neuropsychosis of defense. In J. Strachey et al. (Eds.), *Standard edition* (Vol. 3, p. 176). London: Hogarth Press. (Original work published 1896)

Freud, S. (1981). The ego and the id. In J. Strachey (Ed.), *Standard Edition* (Vol. 5). London: Hogarth Press. (Original work published 1923)

Fromm-Reichman, F. (1959). *Psychoanalysis and psychotherapy.* Chicago: University of Chicago Press.

Furer, M. (1967). Some developmental aspects of the superego. *International Journal of Psychoanalysis, 48,* 277–280.

Garety, P. (1991). Reasoning and delusions. *British Journal of Psychiatry, 15914,* 14–18.

Garfield, D. A. S. (1985). Self-criticism in psychosis. *Dynamic Psychotherapy, 3(2),* 129–144.

Garfield, D. A. S. (1986a). The use of primary process in psychotherapy I: Concrete thinking and the perception of syntax. *Psychotherapy: Theory, Research and Practice, 23(1),* 75–80.

Garfield, D. A. S. (1986b). The use of primary process in psychotherapy II: Transformational. *Psychotherapy: Theory, Research and Practice, 23(4),* 548–555.

Garfield, D. A. S. (1987). The use of primary process in psychotherapy III: Dramatization and the transmission of affect. *Psychotherapy: Theory, Research and Practice, 24(2),* 217–224, 381–386.

Garfield, D. A. S., & Havens, L. (1991). Paranoid phenomena and pathological narcissism. *American Journal of Psychotherapy, XLV(2),* 160–172.

Garfield, D. A. S., & Havens, L. (1993). The treatment of paranoid phenomena: The development of the self. *American Journal of Psychotherapy, 471,* 75–89.

Garfield, D. A. S., & Rapp, C. (1994). Application of artificial intelligence principles to the analysis of "crazy" speech. *Journal of Nervous and Mental Disease, 182(4),* 205–211.

Garfield, D., Rogoff, M. L., & Steinberg, S. (1987). Affect recognition and self-esteem in schizophrenia. *Psychopathology, 20,* 225–233.

Gill, M. (1967). The primary process. *Psychological Issues, 18,* 260–298.

Gill, M. (1982). *Analysis of the transference* (Vol. 1). New York: International Universities Press.

Greenson, R. (1960). Empathy and its vicissitudes. *International Journal of Psychoanalysis, 41,* 418–424.

Greenson, R. (1965). The working alliance and the transference neurosis. *Psychoanalytic Quarterly, 34,* 155–181.

Groves, J. E. (1978). Taking care of the hateful patient. *New England Journal of Medicine, 298*(16), 883–887.

Gunderson, J., Frank, A., Katz, H., Vannicell, M., Frosch, J., & Knapp, P. (1984). Effects of psychotherapy in schizophrenia. II. Comparative outcome of two forms of treatment. *Schizophrenia Bulletin, 10*(4), 564–598.

Gutheil, T., & Havens, L. (1979). The therapeutic alliance: Contemporary meaning and confusions. *International Review of Psycho-Analysis, 6,* 467–481.

Havens, L. (1979). Explorations in the uses of language in psychotherapy: Complex empathic statements. *Psychiatry, 42,* 40–48.

Havens, L. (1986). *Making contact.* Cambridge, MA: Harvard University Press.

Havens, L. (1994). *The function of performative statements.* Unpublished manuscript.

Holt, R. (1962). A critical examination of Freud's concept of bound vs. free cathexis. *Journal of the American Psychoanalytic Association, 10,* 475–525.

Jaspers, K. (1963). *General psychopathology* (J. Hoenig & M. Hamilton, Trans.). Chicago: University of Chicago Press.

Jung, C. G. (1976). The psychogenesis of mental disease. In W. McGuire (Ed.), *The collected works of C. G. Jung* (Vol. 3). Princeton, NJ: Princeton University Press. (Original work published 1907)

Karon, B., & VandenBos, G. (1981). *Psychotherapy of schizophrenia: The treatment of choice.* New York: Jason Aronson.

Kernberg, O. (1976). *Object relations theory and clinical psychoanalysis* (pp. 161–184). New York: Jason Aronson.

Khantzian, E. J., Dalsimer, J. S., & Semrad, E. (1969). The use of interpretation in the psychotherapy of schizophrenia. *American Journal of Psychotherapy, 23*(2), 182–188.

Klein, M. (1930). The psychotherapy of the psychoses. *British Journal of Medicine and Psychology, 10*(1).

Klein, M. (1932). *The psychoanalysis of children.* New York: Grove Press.

Klein, M. (1975). Notes on some schizoid mechanisms. In *Envy and gratitude and other works.* New York: Delacore Press. (Original work published 1946)

Kohut, H. (1971). *The analysis of the self.* New York: International Universities Press.

Kohut, H. (1977). *The restoration of the self.* New York: International Universities Press.

Kraepelin, E. (1903). *Lehrbuch der psychiatrie (7th Ed.)* Leipzig: Barth.

Krystal, J. (1982). The activating aspect of emotions. *Psychoanalysis in Contemporary Thought, 5*(4), 685–642.

Lane, R. D., & Schwartz, G. E. (1987). Levels of emotional awareness: A cognitive-developmental therapy and its application to psychopathology. *American Journal of Psychiatry, 144,* 133–143.

Langs, R. (1976). *The bipersonal field.* New York: Jason Aronson.

Lichtenberg, J. (1989). *Psychoanalysis and motivation.* Hillsdale, NJ: Analytic Press.

Luborsky, L. (1992). *Principles of psychoanalytic psychotherapy.* New York: Basic Books.

Mahler, M. (1972). On the first three subphases of the separation-individuation process. *International Journal of Psychoanalysis, 5f3,* 333–338.

Mann, D. (1986). Six months in a psychiatry treatment of two young chronic schizophrenics. *Psychiatry, 49*(3), 231–240.

Margulies, A., & Havens, L. (1981). The initial encounter: What to do first? *American Journal of Psychiatry, 138*(4), 421–428.

McDougall, J. (1989). *Theaters of the body.* New York: Norton.

Mehlman, R. (1976, February). *Transference, mobilization, transference resolution and the narcissistic alliance.* Paper presented at the Boston Psychoanalytic Society and Institute.

Meissner, W. (1976). A note on internalization as process. *Psychoanalytic Quarterly, 45,* 374–393.

Meissner, W. (1978). *The paranoid process.* New York: Jason Aronson.

Menninger, K. (1952). *A Manual for psychiatric case study.* New York: Grune & Stratton.

Meyer, A. (1951). *The collected papers of Adolf Meyer* (Vol. 2). E. E. Winters (Ed.). Baltimore: Johns Hopkins University Press.

Modell, A. H. (1968). *Object loss and reality.* New York: International Universities Press.

Modell, A. H. (1980). Affects and their non-communication. *International Journal of Psychoanalysis, 61,* 259–267.

Morrison, N. K. (1985). Shame in the treatment of schizophrenia: Theoretical consideration with clinical illustrations. *Yale Journal of Biology and Medicine, 58,* 289–297.

Nemiah, J. (1974). *Denial revisited, reflections on psychosomatic theory.* Paper presented at the 10th European Conference on Psychosomatic Research, Edinburgh, Scotland.

Ortony, A., Clore, G., & Collins, A. (1988). *The cognitive structure of emotions.* Cambridge: Cambridge University Press.

Piaget, J. (1959). *The origins of intelligence in children.* New York: Norton.

Progoff, I. (1973). *Jung, synchronicity, and human destiny.* New York: Delta Books.

Racker, H. (1968). *Transference and countertransference.* New York: International Universities Press.

Rosen, J. (1968). *Direct psychoanalysis.* New York: Grune & Stratton.

Rosenbaum, B., & Sonne, H. (1986). *The language of psychosis.* New York: New York Press.

Rosenfeld, H. (1965). *Psychotic states.* London: Hogarth Press.

Roth, S. (1987). *Psychotherapy: The art of wooing nature.* Narthvale, NJ: Jason Aronson.

Rycroft, C. (1956). The nature and function of the analyst's communication to the patient. *International Journal of Psychoanalysis, 37,* 469–472.

Rycroft, C. (1968). *Imagination and reality.* New York: International Universities Press.

Rycroft, C. (1975). *The innocence of dreams.* New York: Pantheon Press.

Sass, L. (1992). *Madness and modernism.* New York: Basic Books.

Savage, C. (1961). Countertransference in the therapy of schizophrenics. *Psychiatry, 24,* 53–60.

Schafer, R. (1968). *Aspects of internalization.* New York: International Universities Press.

Searles, H. (1965). *Collected papers on schizophrenia and related subjects.* New York: International Universities Press.

Searles, H. (1979). *Countertransference and related subjects.* New York: International Universities Press.

Semrad, E., & Van Buskirk, D. (1969). *Teaching psychotherapy of psychotic patients.* New York: Grune & Stratton.

Shakespeare, W. (1968). The tragedy of Hamlet, Prince of Denmark. In *Shakespeare, The complete works.* New York: Harcourt Brace & World.

Sharpe, E. (1940). Psychophysical problems revealed in language: An examination of metaphor. *International Journal of Psychoanalysis, 21,* 201–213.

Siegelman, E. (1990). *Metaphor and meaning in psychotherapy.* New York: Guilford Press.

Spitz, R. (1957). *No and yes—On the beginning of human communication.* New York: International Universities Press.

Sterba, R. (1934). The fate of the ego in psychoanalytic therapy. *International Journal of Psycho-Analysis, 15,* 117–126.

Stern, D. (1977). *The first relationship: Mother and infant.* Cambridge, MA: Harvard University Press.

Stolorow, R. D., Brandchaft, B., & Atwood, G. E. (1987). The treatment of psychotic states. In R. D. Stolorow, B. Brandchaft, & G. E. Atwood (Eds.),

Psychoanalytic treatment: An intersubjective approach. Hillsdale, NJ: Analytic Press.

Stolorow, R. D., & Lachmann, F. M. (1980). *Psychoanalysis of developmental arrests.* New York: International Universities Press.

Stolorow, R. D., & Stolorow, D. (1987). Affects and selfobjects. In R. D. Stolorow, B. Brandchaft, & G. E. Atwood (Eds.), *Psychoanalytic treatment: An intersubjective approach.* Hillsdale, NJ: Analytic Press.

Sullivan, H. S. (1953). *The interpersonal theory of psychiatry.* New York: Norton.

Sullivan, H. S. (1954). *The psychiatric interview* (p. 64). New York: Norton.

Sullivan, H. S. (1956). *Clinical studies in psychiatry.* New York: Norton.

Taylor, M. A. (1991). The role of the cerebellum in the pathogenesis of schizophrenia. *Neuropsychiatry, neuropsychology and behavioral neurology, 4*(4), 251–280.

Taylor, M. A. (1993). *The neuropsychiatric guide to modern everyday psychiatry.* New York: Free Press.

Thorn, G. W., Adams, R. D., Braunwald, E., Isselbacher, E. J., & Petersdorf, R. L. (Eds.). (1977). *Harrison's principles of internal medicine* (8th ed.). New York: McGraw-Hill.

Tomkins, S. S. (1962). *Affect, imagery, and consciousness.* New York: Springer.

Tomkins. S. S. (1982). Affect theory. In P. Ekman (Ed.), *Emotion in the human face.* Cambridge, U.K.: Cambridge University Press.

Winnicott, D. W. (1947/1975). Hate in the countertransference. In *Collected papers: Through pediatrics to psychoanalysis.* New York: Basic Books.

Winnicott, D. W. (1965). *The maturational processes and the facilitating environment.* London: Hogarth Press.

Wolf, E. (1989). *Treating the self.* New York: Guilford Press.

Wolf, E. (1993). Disruptions of the therapeutic relationship: A view from self psychology. *International Journal of Psychoanalysis, 74*(4), 673–687.

Wurmser, L. (1981). *The mask of shame* (pp. 207–208). Baltimore: Johns Hopkins Press.

Wynne, L. C., & Singer, M. (1963). Thought disorder and family relations of schizophrenics, II. *Archives of General Psychiatry, 9,* 199–206.

Zetzel, E. (1970). *The capacity for emotional growth.* New York: International Universities Press.

AUTHOR INDEX

SUBJECT INDEX